e third time Stan wins The Most Valuable
ayer plaque—presented by the Baseball
riters Assn. (1948)

Honored at a sports dinner in 1951—Sta
Musial, Dick McBride (college grid star) an
Phil Rizzuto of the Yankees

vo "greats"—Stan Musial and Ted Williams
the Boston Red Sox

Stan Musial and Eddie Stanky

vo leading hitters of the National League—
an with Duke Snider of the Dodgers

Willie Mays, Ted Kluszewski, Stan Musial

Stan Musial and Frank J. Shaughnessy.
Musial receives award as "Best Player of
the Year," presented by N. Y. Chapter of
the Baseball Writers Assn. (1947)

Cardinal rookie in 1942

Musial shows his form during a Florida workout

Stan the Man

Stan with his mother, Mrs. Mary Musial

Papa and Mamma Musial with their childre Janey, Jerry and Dickie

THE
STAN MUSIAL STORY

BY GENE SCHOOR
WITH HENRY GILFOND

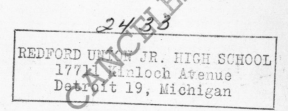

JULIAN MESSNER, INC. · NEW YORK

Published by Julian Messner, Inc.
8 West 40th Street, New York 18
Published simultaneously in Canada
by The Copp Clark Company, Ltd.
Copyright 1955 by Gene Schoor
Printed in the United States of America

Library of Congress Catalog Card No. 55-6929

ACKNOWLEDGMENT

In appreciation for their help in the preparation of the manuscript for THE STAN MUSIAL STORY, many thanks to Paul Schoenstein of the *Journal-American*, Ike Gellis of the *New York Post*, Charles Shapiro, Fran Schoor, Sandy Rosenberg, Tess Palmer, Edna Gilbert, and to Associated Press Photos, International News Photos, Wide World Photos.

To Rebecca Estey, my senior year teacher at Passaic High School, in New Jersey, without whose sympathetic understanding this book would never have been written

THE STAN MUSIAL STORY

Billy Southworth, fighting manager of the pennant-contending St. Louis Cardinals, pushed his way into the clubhouse.

"Out on the field in twenty minutes!" he yelled to his players who were already stripping for that quick shower between games of the double-header.

He slapped the back of his rookie pitcher Howie Pollet. "Good game, Howie. You pitched a nice game today, and that curve ball was working like a charm."

Then, flanked by his two top coaches Mike Gonzalez and Buzzy Wares, the St. Louis pilot dropped exhausted into his chair. "That was too close," he said, pulling off his cap and wiping the sweat from his forehead.

"We won it," said Gonzalez quietly.

"Sure," said Southworth, looking out anxiously at his exhausted ballplayers. "But we've got to win them all."

He flipped the dial of the radio to the Dodger game. The Dodgers were in first place but St. Louis was snapping at their heels, a game behind.

"If the Dodgers lose today," offered Buzzy Wares hopefully, "we take over first place."

"Sure, sure!" snapped the scrappy manager. "And if we win them all we've got the pennant."

The voice of crack baseball announcer Red Barber filtered through. "Pittsburgh leading three to one and the Dodgers just three outs from losing this big one. Every game is a big one now. Here's the pitch," Barber's voice was tense with excitement. "Galan swings, drives one high against the wall and goes into second base standing up."

"There she goes," spit Southworth under his breath. "That's the ball game." He turned on Mike Gonzalez. "We're pitching Max Lanier in this second game. Think I'll pull Terry Moore. He didn't do a thing for us out there today."

Barber's excited voice filtered through again. "It's a line drive single over short. Galan scores easily and Peewee Reese is safe on first base. And those battling Brooks are going at it again."

"Turn that radio off!" snapped Billy Southworth, but nobody moved. "I'm going to use that youngster Musial, that's what I'll do—Musial for Terry Moore in the second game."

Terry Moore, a great Cardinal outfielder for years, had been hit by a pitched ball and suffered a concussion. Ordinarily, he would have been out for the rest of the season, but St. Louis was in one of the tightest pennant races in the history of the National League. It was September 18th and only a game and a half separated the Cardinals from the league-leading Dodgers. It was closer than that. Both clubs were tied in the games-lost column. If the Cardinals won the last fourteen games of their scheduled one hundred and fifty-four games, they could do no worse than tie for the league championship. Both teams were tense and anxious as they battled each other for that big World Series opportunity. Terry Moore made his first appearance at the bat in almost a month, but he had not fully recovered from his injuries, and he proved no great help with his bat.

The Cardinals won it, all right. Howie Pollet, the brilliant rookie, came up with his fourth straight win, but it took an eighth-inning rally and a couple of home runs by the veteran Estel Crabtree to overcome an early Boston lead. Billy Southworth took the victory well enough, but the fighting manager who had come to the Cardinals just the year before—in the middle of the 1940 season, to pull the St. Louis club out of seventh place and into the contending third slot in the league standings—was going to settle for nothing less than the pennant in 1941.

"Get Terry Moore," ordered Billy Southworth.

Buzzy Wares went out to get the star center fielder, as Southworth turned his attention once more to the radio report of the Dodger game.

"It's a high, hard line drive heading for the center field gates," drawled Red Barber. "Vince DiMaggio is chasing it, but he'll never get it. Reese has scored. Herman is scoring and Pete Reiser is safe at third base. The score is now: Dodgers four, Pittsburgh Pirates three. And that's all for Ken Heintzelman. Here comes the Pirate manager, and Luke Sewell is coming in to pitch for Pittsburgh."

"About time!" snapped Mike Gonzales.

Bill Southworth didn't say anything. Terry Moore was in the room.

"You want to see me?" he asked.

"Yeah," said Southworth. "Nice game you played."

"Thanks," said Moore, "but I didn't hit anything."

"You will," said the Card manager.

"Sure," said Terry. "I always could hit Tobin."

Jim Tobin was scheduled to pitch the second game of the double-header for Casey Stengel's Braves.

"I've been thinking you ought to sit this one out," said Southworth.

"You need me in there," said Moore.

"There are twelve more games after this one," said

Southworth. "We'll need you for every one of them. But you've had enough today."

Terry Moore shuffled his feet uneasily. He didn't want to miss a second of the fight to the wire for the pennant.

"You're still tired," said Southworth. "You don't come back so fast after you've been beaned by a pitch the way you were. Matter of fact, I wouldn't be using you at all if we weren't chasing to catch up with the Dodgers."

Terry Moore gritted his teeth. He knew his manager was right. He was tired, all right, but he could play if he had to.

"Who are you going to put out in center field instead of me?" he asked.

"We'll put Johnny Hopp in center," said Billy South-worth. Terry Moore was one man on his club who de-served an explanation of team strategy. He had earned it. "We'll move Crabtree over to right field."

"How about left field?" asked Moore.

"We've got that big kid from Rochester."

Mike Gonzales and Buzzy Wares looked questioningly at each other.

"He hit pretty well for the Red Wings," said Terry Moore.

"And he was the home run champion with Springfield," offered Buzzy Wares.

"A lot of them come up from the bushes with a big batting average and can't hit big-league pitching for nothing," countered Mike Gonzales.

"Sure," said the thoughtful Cardinal manager. "But Terry isn't going to play in this second game and we've got to find out about this kid sooner or later."

He looked around at his coaches and Terry for an opinion. There was none coming.

"Bring the youngster in," he ordered, and Buzzy Wares went out to bring in the youngster fresh out of the International League team, the Rochester Red Wings.

He was a big blond fellow and he looked like a ballplayer. But a lot of men look like ballplayers and there the resemblance ends. Although he was only twenty, he looked younger. Four months ago he had been playing for the Springfield club. It was only a matter of weeks that he had played ball for a Triple A club, and now he had been catapulted suddenly into the major leagues, and with a team which was going down to the finish line—neck and neck with the leading Brooklyn Dodgers.

"You're playing left field," said Billy Southworth. "You're playing left field in this second game with Boston."

The youngster knew he was supposed to say something but he didn't know just what to say. All he could do was to shake his head in acknowledgement.

"You know how to play that left field wall," said the St. Louis Red Bird manager. "You've been out there practicing."

"Yes, sir," said the youngster.

"All right," said Billy Southworth. "Remember that this Boston pitcher Jim Tobin was a busher himself. He's just another ballplayer throwing them in to the plate, and it's just a baseball he's throwing up at you, nothing else. If you could hit them for Rochester, you can hit them for us. You want to remember that."

"Yes, sir," said the rookie.

Southworth looked the kid over. There was a lot more he wanted to say to him but there wasn't time. Besides, the Red Bird manager was pretty tired. He needed the next few minutes before the second game started to get a few precious seconds of complete rest.

"That's all," he said. "Now get out on the field and let's see what you can do!"

In 1941 Jim Tobin was one of baseball's top pitchers. In the first two innings of that memorable second game of the September 18th double-header, he set down the snarling Cardinals in order. He got Marty Marion and Gus Mancuso for easy outs in the third inning. Max Lanier got to first on a scratch single. Johnny Hopp walked. There were Cardinals on first and second when the youngster from Rochester stepped up to the plate.

Ray Berres, the Boston Braves catcher, called time and walked out to the pitcher's mound.

"Don't give him a good pitch," he said to Jim Tobin. "They say he hit them a mile for Rochester."

"Sure," said Tobin. "And so did a lot of other guys. This is the big league. The pitching is a little different."

"Sure, sure," said Berres. "Probably never saw a curve."

"May be he never even saw a fast ball."

Berres smiled. It's the job of the catcher to keep his pitcher loose and easy, on an even keel, confident.

"Just don't give him anything to hit. Keep him off balance, guessing!"

Meanwhile, the youngster kept his own council. He glanced up at the big crowd in St. Louis' Sportsman's Park. He looked at his manager for a signal.

"Get a piece of it!" yelled Southworth.

The kid took his stance at the plate. Max Lanier took his lead off second. Johnny Hopp edged off first. Jim Tobin, with two men on base, wasn't taking a full windup. He brought the ball down to his chest, then hurled a fast ball.

"Ball one!" howled umpire Bill Reardon.

"That's the eye," yelled Johnny Mize from the Cardinal bench.

"Get a piece of it!" yelled Southworth again.

Jim Tobin looked at Lanier off second, Johnny Hopp off first. He brought his hands to the stop position, then threw to the plate. The twenty-year-old rookie from Rochester swung, hammered the ball on a line for the right field wall while the stadium rocked to the roar of the fans, as Max Lanier and Johnny Hopp raced across the plate. The kid from Rochester, a smile on his face, stood safely perched on second base with his first major league hit, a ringing double that scored two runs.

Jim Tobin pitched a magnificent game that afternoon, giving up only six hits. Jimmy Brown, Cardinal third baseman, got one of them, Estel Crabtree one, Creepy Crespi one, Max Lanier a scratch single and the kid from the Rochester Red Wings blasted two. And it was the rookie's double, scoring two runs, which spelled the difference in the ball game, St. Louis winning it by the score of three to two, and shaving a half game off the lead of the Brooklyn Dodgers.

"The kid's all right," said Terry Moore in the clubhouse.

"Great!" said Mike Gonzales.

Billy Southworth was quiet but more meaningful.

"You came through for the club like a big-leaguer," he said, slapping the youngster's back. "I want you out there in left field tomorrow."

The twenty-year-old rookie would be out there in the field tomorrow, all right. He was going to be out on the field for the St. Louis Cardinals from then on, for as long as the Red Bird manager could keep him playing.

The twenty-year-old rookie from the Rochester Red Wings was Stanley Frank Musial, and that double against the stellar pitching of Jim Tobin was his announcement that a new star had made his initial appearance in the baseball world.

CHAPTER 2

The tall, lean, blond youngster, his baseball mitt tucked into his hip pocket, raced down the school steps and hurried off toward Donora's Legion Field. This was going to be the first game of the 1938 season and the high school pitcher was eager to get down to the diamond. It wasn't his first game, nor his first chance to show how he could pitch. As a matter of fact, the young high school southpaw couldn't remember when he hadn't played ball. He was thirteen when he had been drafted into sandlot games with young men of nineteen and twenty. He had even played ball with Donora's American Steel and Wire Company ball club. The kid pitcher was almost a veteran, considering all the games he had been in. Still, every game was a new one for him, a new experience, with all the excitement and the competition, and the kid was in a hurry to get into his uniform.

"Hey, Stan!"

Musial scarcely broke his stride.

"C'mon, Ed!" he yelled over his shoulder.

Ed Pado, the Donora high school right fielder, quickened his pace, broke into a trot.

"What's your hurry? We've got plenty of time."

"Told Coach Duda I'd be down early," he explained.

"You're plenty early," said Ed, catching his breath.

Bill Olenic, slugging shortshop of the Donora High Dragons, joined them. So did Pete Peskor, the Donora catcher.

"What's the rush?" queried Pete.

"Stan's afraid he'll miss the train."

They all laughed. There was no train to catch. Donora was a comparatively poor town and couldn't afford to send its ball clubs any distance from home. Besides, baseball was not an important sport at Donora High. The big sport for that school of four hundred fifty boys and girls was football. Baseball had been just something to fill in the slack of athletic activities until the next football season.

"Think there'll be anyone out there to watch us?" asked Stan.

"Are you kidding?" asked Olenic. "Half the town will be coming to see you pitch!"

"Sure," said Stan, skeptically.

"And the other half will be coming to see you smack the ball out of the park," added Ed Pado.

Stan Musial smiled. He felt that the boys were kidding him. But they weren't. Maybe the whole town wouldn't turn out to watch the young southpaw star on the diamond, but never before in its history had the people of Donora shown such a lively interest in baseball.

"That kid's got more speed on the ball than anyone I've ever seen—and I've seen some good pitching," offered one of the local fans. "That includes big-league stars like Claude Passeau who's pitching for Philadelphia, and Bucky Walters who's pitching for the Cincinnati Redlegs."

Maybe the Donora fan was exaggerating a little, and maybe the fan who thought Stan was as great a batter as he had ever seen was painting too bright a picture. But that is the way the baseball fever gets hold of a town. Some youngster comes along and electrifies the fans with his sensational natural ability and the neighbors go all-out in praise of the ballplayer, and the game itself becomes the biggest thing in town. That's the way it was with young Stan Musial. He was a natural-born ballplayer and the crowd recognized it. Suddenly Donora became baseball crazy. There was a good-sized crowd out to see Donora's first game against the more powerful Monessen High.

"You can beat them," said Coach Mike Duda to his Donora Dragons. "We've got a hard-hitting, fast, aggressive team. And Stan, we're counting on you to blow that fast ball right by those big boys from Monessen. Beat them, and the town will be ours. Now get out there and play them off their feet!" "Remember," he added, "the first game is a big one. Beat Monessen and baseball becomes the big sport in Donora."

He glanced at Jim Russell who was sitting on the bench. Jim Russell was head of all athletics at Donora High. Jim was strictly a football man. He had played football at Notre Dame with such All-American stars as Frank Leahy, Marty Brill, Johnny Law. He had been a star on his own, coached by the immortal Knute Rockne. It was Rockne who had secured the coaching berth for Russell at Donora. Coach Mike Duda knew this, but he kept talking baseball just the same in order to build his boys up.

"I want you to get in there now and beat the tar out of these fellows from Monessen," he repeated. "And I know you can do it."

Russell smiled at his baseball coach. He approved the pep talk. He liked to see his school win. He even added his own few words of encouragement. "You can do it, fellows. We licked them in football. You can do it on the diamond."

Oslowski was first man up for the Donora team, and he was safe on first when the nervous Monessen shortstop fumbled the ball. Bill Olenic immediately showed the power on the Dragons squad by driving out a home run. Guffey was safe on another error. Joe Dzik lined to third but Guffey scrambled back to first base safely. Pete Peskor walked, sending Joe Dzik to second, and Stan Musial stepped to the plate.

"Watch that boy hit!" said Coach Duda, excitedly.

"Big enough to be a top football player," said Jim Russell.

"I like the way he swings," said Mike Duda. "He's a natural, if I ever saw one."

Stan took the first pitch, then stepped into a curve and laced it on a line between the Monessen right and center fielders for a clean double. Guffey scored and Pete Peskor stopped at third.

"Attaboy, Stan!" yelled Coach Duda. "Great ballplayer, that youngster," he said to Jim Russell. "Wait till you see him pitch!"

Jim Russell was impressed, all right, but not the way Mike Duda expected him to be.

"I'd like to see that boy in a football uniform." he said.

Stan was a left-handed pitcher. A lefthander is supposed to be erratic. But there was nothing erratic about Musial's pitching that afternoon.

Susko, Levitsky and Kunsa came up to bat in Monessen's first inning, and Stan dazzled them with his speed. He was so fast that Pete Peskor, his catcher, had trouble holding onto his pitches. The Monessen boys swung viciously but with complete futility. Stan came back to the bench at the end of the first inning with three quick strike-outs.

"What did I tell you!" exclaimed Coach Mike Duda.

"He's all right," said Jim Russel, his interest growing.

He motioned to the youngster.

"How come I've never seen you out for football?" he asked.

"I guess I've never been out," answered Stan simply.

"You've got a good arm," said Russell. "We could use you in the backfield. We could use a strong arm like yours. We need a good forward passer."

Seven times the Monessen ball team came up to bat —twenty-six men in all—as Stan limited them to three hits, two bases on balls and a lonely run. The big thing, however, was the way Musial mowed down the opposition. Of the twenty-one put-outs, the brilliant southpaw hurler was responsible for seventeen. Seventeen men came up to the plate to be cut down on strikes. There were only four put-outs on balls hit to the outfield. It was a phenomenal exhibition, an average of better than two strike-out victims for every inning of the ball game. Musial had just blown Monessen down to bring home Donora's first victory, and Coach Duda, along with all the other boys on the team, pounded the youngster's back, excited by their first and most important conquest.

"Great, Stan! Great!" yelled Duda.

He turned to Jim Russell.

"What did I tell you?" he demanded.

Jim Russell smiled.

"You're all right," he said to Stan. "I'll be expecting you down for football. We need men like you for Donora."

Stan didn't answer right off and Jim Russell turned away. The truth of the matter was that Stan didn't want to play football. It wasn't that he didn't like the game. It wasn't that he didn't enjoy getting into a practice scrimmage every once in a while, but he just didn't want to get involved in the gridiron game full time. He wanted to play baseball.

Bill Olenic and Eugene Norton, two of the Donora Dragons, cornered Stan on the way home.

"Coach Russell sure is sold on you," said Norton.

"Going out for football?" asked Bill Olenic.

They both knew how Stan felt about it. They wondered how he was going to resist the pressure.

"I don't know," said Stan.

"A lot of guys have been All-American football players and then played big-league baseball," offered Norton. "At least, that's what Russell is going to tell you."

"I know," said Stan.

He looked at his two pals for some assistance.

"You've got to go to college to play football."

"What's the matter with college?" asked Olenic.

"Nothing," said Stan, "except that my father works in the mill and there are a lot of kids in the house, and I feel that I ought to be making a little money soon. Got to help Dad and the family."

"Playing baseball?" asked Norton.

"Yes, playing baseball!" said Stan.

The three young ballplayers were thoughtful for a minute.

"You can do it," said Bill Olenic finally.

"Good luck!" added Gene Norton.

They shook hands, meaningfully, then went their separate ways, each with his problem and his own dream.

CHAPTER 3

Stan hadn't played football for Donora High, but he had been one of the star players on the basketball team. He had developed a terrific hook shot, and it was his aggressive and smart playing which had catapulted Donora, unbeaten, into the game for the sectional title against the powerful Harbrack High five.

Dick Ercius played center for the Dragons. Gene Norton, of the baseball nine, was another star basketball player. The other regulars were George Kosko, Bob Garcia and, of course, Stan Musial. They had beaten Washington, Uniontown, Monessen, Charleroi and Brownsville, among others. They were a confident team as they took the floor for the title game against Harbrack.

It was a rough and tough game, and when the whistle blew at the end of the regulation game, the big crowd let out a mighty yell, for both squads had played their hearts out for the coveted championship—and the game had ended in a flat tie.

There was the usual rest period and then they were at it again in that extra period which is always the most dramatic of any basketball game. It's do or die, and that's the way the boys played it.

Dick Ercius got the jump. George Kosko dribbled the ball toward the Harbrack basket. He passed to Bob Garcia. Bob Garcia tossed to Gene Norton and Norton whipped the ball to Stan Musial who was moving past the basket and away. Stan had the ball. He kept going, turned, hooked the ball for the basket, then went crashing into the wall. The basket was good. Donora High was in the lead, but Stan was down on the floor with a deadening ache in his left shoulder.

"Nothing," he said to the coach who was kneeling beside him. "It's just a bruise."

He continued to play, but the hook shot became increasingly painful and more difficult. Harbrack won that game and the championship. Stan never complained about the injury to his left shoulder, but there would come a day when he would remember it, for it was to prove the turning point in one of the most amazing stories of baseball's stars.

Stan didn't worry about that arm in the season of 1938. There seemed to be no need to worry. That left arm was making history in Donora, and Donora was suddenly becoming baseball conscious. The fantastic pitching and batting of Stan Musial was making Donora forget every other sport.

At the American Steel and Wire Company, where most of the men of the small town worked, Lukasz Musial, Polish immigrant father of the fabulous Stan Musial, abruptly found himself the center of all kinds of attention—a hero by proxy.

"That boy of yours is some pitcher."

"That Stanley of yours is some hitter. He can hit the ball a mile."

Lukasz felt great pride in the adulation bestowed on his son, but he was a little embarrassed. He loved America to which he had migrated in search of freedom, a better life for himself and for his family, but he had never had time to familiarize himself with all of the facets of American life. To him football and basketball and baseball were games you played for fun, and he was happy that his son Stan was enjoying them. However, he couldn't understand hero worship in connection with sports. When his fellow workers raved he merely grinned, thinking, let him enjoy himself while he's young. Soon he'll be working in the mill unless I can afford to send him to college.

"He's a good boy," he said modestly. "My Stanley is a good boy."

"Sure is," echoed the workers at the mill, thinking of Stan's power at the plate and on the pitching mound, and hoping the son of the Polish immigrant would be displaying the same prowess on the gridiron, for they understood football better than baseball, since it was closer to the European game of soccer.

Stan, however, tried to keep football out of his mind. He concentrated on his baseball. He had a pretty good evaluation of his ability as a ballplayer, and he knew that he had more than a fighting chance to carve a niche for himself in baseball than in football. The sudden appearance of strangers in the stands to watch the Donora Dragons play ball helped sharpen the dreams of the youngster.

"That's Johnny Gooch," said Coach Mike Duda, pointing out one of the men. "He's a big-league baseball scout. Pie Traynor must have sent him down to look a couple of you boys over for the Pittsburgh Pirates."

Another time it was Bill Rheinhardt who had a job coaching at George Washington College, but also found time to scout for the New York Yankees. Another time it was Andy French, business manager for the St. Louis Cardinal farm team in Monessen. They all took a good look and they were interested.

In Donora High's second game Stan didn't pitch. He

played the otufield, went to the plate three times and belted two doubles for the Dragons. He sparked the Donora 9-0 win over Rostraver High.

In a return game with Rostrover, Stan took over the hurling assignment and allowed only two hits while striking out fourteen in the regulation seven-inning game for an easy 22-3 victory. Rostraver's three runs came in as a result of some loose fielding and all on errors.

Against Charleroi, Stan was brought into the box in relief of the faltering Donora hurler. Charleroi had scored four times and the bases were full in the third inning with none out when the star southpaw took over. And all he did was retire the side in order, allow one hit and one run for the rest of the game and strike out ten men en route. Donora lost that game 5-1, but Stan was brilliant in relief. Baseball scout Andy French of the St. Louis Cardinals, who was watching that game, didn't need any more proof of the youngster's ability. He went directly to the Musial household to proposition Papa Lukasz on a baseball contract for his son Stanley. Papa Lukasz would have to do the signing, since Stan was under age, and it was here that Andy French ran up against an unexpected obstacle.

"I want my boy to go to college," said Papa Lukasz. "I want him to get the best of everything in America. In Poland a steel worker's son couldn't go to college. In America he can. I want Stanley to go to college."

"But he can make a great career for himself," offered Andy French. "And he can make a lot of money. He will be a big man in baseball."

"Stanley is going to college. I want him to be a professional man. I don't want him to spend his life playing games."

French left the Musial home in a sweat, but he came

around to watch Stan play again. What he saw made him more determined than ever to get young Musial's name on a baseball contract.

In his fifth game of the season, against Monongahela, Stan banged out two hits, a slashing double and a bases-full home run. The Monongahela pitcher walked him twice in this game, but in the fifth inning Stan came up with the bases loaded and drove the ball for a tremendous four-hundred-foot home run. It was a thrilling blast. It had the fans standing and cheering. It had Andy French hot under the collar that he couldn't sign the boy up then and there. He was worried sick that someone else was going to beat him to it.

Stan cracked three hits in four trips to the plate against East Pike Run High School. Against California High School Stan got two hits in addition to pitching masterful ball, giving up two hits while striking out fourteen.

The story was pretty much the same throughout the season. Young Musial kept striking them out whenever he pitched, and his hitting was good enough to give him the schoolboy championship with a dazzling batting average of .380.

Andy French wasn't giving up on his drive to sign up the youngster, making all sorts of fancy offers to both Stan and his father. Jim Russell worked just as hard trying to get Stan out for football. He matched Andy French's offers with some dazzling offers of his own. French's propositions, of course, met with young Musial's immediate approval. Andy didn't have to offer much to get Stan to join the professional baseball fraternity. Russell's ideas, however, fell in line with Papa Lukasz's dreams for his son. Stan was torn between his love for baseball and a great desire to please his father.

4

"Sure, I know how you feel about baseball," said Coach Jim Russell to the perplexed Stan Musial sitting on the other side of his desk in the school athletic office. "And I'm with you all the way, Stan. You understand that, don't you?"

"Yes, sir," said Stan.

"I've watched you play every game," continued the football coach, "and you're great. You're a natural. You've got the speed, the stamina, the co-ordination, the intelligence—everything that's needed to make a great athlete. And you'll be as great in football as you've ever been in basketball and baseball."

"Thanks, Coach."

"I mean every word of it," said the coach. "That's why I want you out for football. That's why I won't take 'no' for an answer."

Stan was quiet. He played with the cap in his hand.

"Jim Thorpe was one of the greatest football players of all time," argued Russell. "He made All-America every time he played for those Carlisle Indians. And he was good enough for John McGraw and the New York Giants."

"I know," said Stan.

"Look at Christy Mathewson," continued Russell. "You're a pitcher. I don't have to tell you that Mathewson was the greatest pitcher baseball ever had, do I?"

"No, sir."

"Do you know what he did for Bucknell?"

"Played football."

"He sure did! He was the greatest gridder Bucknell ever had."

"What makes you so stubborn?" asked Coach Russell. "Play football for Donora and we'll get you a football scholarship for half a dozen colleges. Might even get you a scholarship to Notre Dame. You'd like that, wouldn't you?"

Musial hesitated. He was being offered a priceless opportunity to play football. It was the kind of opportunity that Papa Musial prayed for.

"What do you say, Stan?" persisted the football coach.

Stan said nothing. As far as he was concerned the glory picture Russell painted had no meaning for him at all. Baseball was his game and no college scholarship, no All-America, could make him change his mind.

"You talked this over with your dad?" asked Russell.

Stan nodded. "Yes, sir."

"And what does your dad say?"

"He wants me to go to college," said Stan simply.

"And he's right," snapped Russell. "He knows what he's talking about! You listen to your father, Stan. You couldn't get any better advice anywhere. And you tell him we'll get you to college on a full scholarship, too! It won't cost him or you a cent for the best education you can get anywhere in the world!"

The interview was over. As far as the coach was concerned the struggle was over, too. Stan was going to play football for Donora.

Musial wasn't sure. He knew how his father was going to react to a scholarship offer. It was going to be practically impossible to beat that argument from Papa Lukasz's point of view. Sure he would still say his boy was playing games, but if playing these games meant an opportunity for education, for a chance at a good profession, well, that was different. If Papa said "football," Stan knew it was going to be football. Still he could try just once more to get Papa to understand what baseball meant to him.

"Talk it over with your dad," said Russell, walking Stan to the door of his office.

"I will," said Stan. He closed the door behind him and stood for a moment in the school corridor wondering whether he would have to destroy the good feeling at home by insisting that he had a right to his own ambition —or whether he would just have to forget baseball forever.

With a heavy heart he walked slowly toward the doors of the high school. He passed the library, stopped for a moment, then turned back. Through the windows of the library door he could see Miss Klotz busily sorting cards and books at her desk. He opened the door and walked in.

"Why, Stanley!" Miss Klotz put down her cards and motioned him to a seat beside her.

She was one of those teachers who really loved the boys and girls and they recognized it. She was the kind of woman they could talk to. She had a sympathetic ear and she understood the importance of their problems. The young people came to her for advice and she could be counted on for an honest opinion and real help.

"You look troubled, Stanley," she said. "Something bothering you?"

"Nothing terribly important," said young Musial.

"Of course not," said Miss Klotz. "But let's have it anyway."

And Stan spilled it all—the way he felt about baseball, Jim Russell's offers, the pressure at home.

"I really don't know what to do, Miss Klotz."

"But it seems to me," countered the sympathetic school librarian, "that you know exactly what you want to do. You want to play baseball. It's as simple as that! Make up your mind, Stanley. Then stick to your guns. Don't back down from your own decision."

Stan looked up at her. This was the first cheerful note he had heard in a long while.

"You mean," he asked, "that I should forget all about football? Forget everything about Coach Russell and those scholarship offers?"

"That's the way you'd like it, isn't it?" asked Miss Klotz.

"Sure," said Stan.

He hesitated a moment, fumbled with his cap again. "But how about my father?"

"I think your father will understand."

"But he doesn't," he said frowning.

Stan sat down again.

"Look here, Stanley," began Miss Klotz, "no father is going to say 'no' to a son's ambition, if the ambition is a good and honest one. Maybe your father doesn't understand what you're after. Maybe you haven't convinced him. Baseball is just a game to most people. They don't understand it as a career, an important career. You've got the facts and figures. Why don't you give them to him?"

There was something infectious about Miss Klotz's enthusiasm. She could raise flagging spirits the way a coach can lift his ball team with a pep speech. And she had put her finger on Stanley's faltering courage.

"Maybe you're right," said Stanley. "I'll talk to him. I'll convince him. And I can do it!"

"I'm sure you can," Miss Klotz said, smiling for the

first time that afternoon. "And if you need any help, just ask me to your house. Maybe I can tell your father a thing or two he doesn't know."

Stan laughed.

"I'm sure you can. Gee, Miss Klotz! You know, you're great. Thanks a lot."

He started for home and the big conflict with all the confidence in the world. But he didn't go straight home. There was one more person he had to see before talking to his father.

CHAPTER 5

Mr. Labash, who ran the most popular grocery store in Donora, looked up from his counter as young Stan Musial came in through the door. Stan worked for Mr. Labash after school, on holidays and during the summer vacations, but the grocer knew that young Musial wasn't coming in to work this afternoon.

"You're looking for Lillian?" he asked, when the formal greetings were over. Lillian was his young and pretty daughter. She and Stan had been childhood sweethearts and Mr. Labash approved of the good-looking, easy-going and thoroughly likeable Stan Musial. "She's in the back of the store," said Mr. Labash. "Do you want me to call her?"

Stan smiled back at the grinning storekeeper. They understood each other pretty well.

"I'll find her," said young Musial.

"I'm sure you will," said Mr. Labash. He was still grinning as Stan moved in behind the counters to the door leading to the back room.

Lillian and Stanley were still kids, but their outlook was quite mature. Struggle and poverty had given them an adult understanding of life and its attendant problems. They meant to make a life of their own as soon as possible.

"College is going to take at least four years," said Stan. "We're not going to wait four years to get married and have a life of our own. It isn't fair to you. It isn't fair to me. I've been offered a baseball contract with the Cardinal club. There are other clubs that want me, too," said Stan. "It won't pay much in the beginning. Maybe I won't get more than ninety or a hundred dollars a month. I know it's not a lot of money, but it's enough for us to get married, for a start, anyhow."

Lillian didn't say anything. She just listened. She loved Stan and wanted to get married just as much as he did, but she also knew what the chances were for a man with a college degree and she didn't want to stand in the way of Stan's future.

"I know what you're thinking," he said, taking her hand, "but I'm not giving up anything. There's only one thing I care for more than baseball, and I don't have to tell you what that is."

"I know, Stan," she said, fighting back the tears, "but I don't want you ever to feel sorry. I don't want you ever to feel you made a mistake."

"I'm not making any mistake," he insisted. "I just want to know that you're with me. I've just got to have you with me all the time, Lillian."

He held her close to him. "I'm going to play ball," said Stan. "I'm going to be a great ballplayer, Lillian. I'm going to be playing way up there in the big leagues, for you and for me."

Stan ran all the way home. He was anxious to put the whole question on the line for the last time. He was ready to argue his cause as he had never argued it before, and he had to convince his father that baseball was going to be his job and his career.

Lukasz Musial was not sitting in his favorite armchair when Stan entered the house. He was pacing the floor, disturbed and angry, and in the armchair sat the St. Louis Cardinals scout Andy French.

"I'm a good American," Papa Lukasz was saying forcibly. "I am the foreman in the American Steel and Wire Company. I have raised four daughters—they are all older than Stanley—and two boys. I don't want a stranger to come into my house to tell me that I am not doing right by my children."

"I didn't say you're not doing right by your children," protested Andy French quietly. "All I said was that you're not doing right by Stan."

Papa Lukasz turned on his son.

"Do you hear what he is saying, Stanley? Is this right, Stanley? Have I been a good father to you, or haven't I?"

Stan, stunned by the unexpected scene on his arrival, just looked at the two men.

"Tell him!" insisted Papa Lukasz. "Have I been as good a father to you as I could be? Have I given you everything I could give you?"

"Yes, Papa," said Stan quietly.

"I know we've had very little money. We are not rich with all the good things you can buy at the stores. But we have been a good family. We love our children. Our children love us. We have done everything we could for them."

Andy French was used to emotional scenes on the ball field. He could battle it out with any man on the diamond. But this was a different situation and he couldn't cope with it.

"You don't understand, Mr. Musial," he argued. "Baseball is the biggest game in America. It's really a fine profession for a young man today. He can win all kinds of glory—and money, too. Look at Lou Gehrig. Look at Babe Ruth. Babe Ruth was an orphan and he became the greatest sports hero in America."

"These are only names," countered Papa. "I don't know Lou Gehrig or Babe Ruth. All I know is that I want my boy to go to college. I want him to become a professional man, a doctor, a lawyer, a teacher. I don't want him to work in the mills."

"But he won't have to work in the mills," said French. "We'll give him a hundred dollars a month, just to start with. He can work himself up to a fine salary, if he's good, and I know he is good. He can make a real future for himself and his family. Baseball is a big business."

Papa Lukasz was impressed by the salary and the promise of the future, but not quite enough. "It is still a game, and nothing else—a game for boys."

"You're wrong, Pa," Stanley found his tongue at last. "Baseball is a profession, Pa, just like being a lawyer or a doctor or an engineer."

"Maybe," said Papa Lukasz, "but I don't understand it."

"Come on, Papa, sign the contract for your boy's sake," put in Andy French eagerly.

Papa thought for a moment as he paced the floor.

"I want to play ball, Papa," added Stan, but all of his assurance was gone now. "I want to play ball more than anything else in the world."

Papa Lukasz stopped abruptly. He turned on his son. "You're a young boy," he said sharply. "You don't know what is best for you."

Andy French bent to pick up his brief case. Papa Lukasz was too set in his ways. There was no sense in battling any more. He had lost and he was ready to say goodby to the Musials and forget all about them.

"Too bad," he said quietly. "That son of yours had the makings of a great star."

Papa Lukasz didn't hear him. He was looking at his son standing there with tears pouring down his face.

"You're crying," said Papa Lukasz, softening quickly.

Stan shook his head.

"I'm not crying," he said.

"But you are crying," insisted Papa Lukasz, fighting the tears coming into his own eyes.

Papa Lukasz loved his children. He would suffer any torment to save them torment, any pain to save them pain.

"This baseball means so much to you?" he asked unhappily. "This game is so important that you cry? I never see you cry before Stanley."

"It means everything," said Stan.

Papa turned to Andy French.

"Maybe I don't understand," he said, bewildered. "Maybe I am wrong."

"Then you'll sign?" said the Cardinal scout, puzzled by the sudden change in Mr. Musial, still unsure.

"You want me to sign?" asked Papa of Stanley.

Stan nodded his head slowly.

Papa brushed the tears from his eyes.

"Where are the papers, Mr. French," he asked.

"You're not making a mistake, Mr. Musial," said Andy, by now close to tears himself.

"I hope you are right. I hope you are both right," said Papa Lukasz.

He called in his wife Mary.

"Stanley is going to be a baseball player. I'm going to sign the contract with Mr. French."

"You know what's best, Papa," said Mama Musial.

Ever since they had met in the Donora mill, where Mary had sorted nails and Lukasz, only twenty years old, had pushed around one hundred-pound bundles of American steel wire, Mama Musial knew that what Papa did was right.

"You'll be happy, Stanley," she said to her son, putting her arms around him.

"It's what I want most, Mama," said Stan, wiping away his tears.

They watched Papa Lukasz sign the papers, and before the summer was out, Stan Musial was wearing the uniform of the Williamson baseball club in the small but very much alive Mountain States League in West Virginia.

CHAPTER 6

Pittsburgh was only twenty-eight miles from Donora, and the Donora sports editor John Bunardzya had promised Stan a trip to Forbes Field to see the great Pittsburgh Pirates ball club in action. It was Stan's first visit to a big-league game. The Pirates were in action against the great New York Giants and Musial watched the flawless performance of the great big-league stars.

"Someday soon, Johnny," said young Stan Musial, "I'm going to be a ballplayer on a big-league team, like the Giants or the Pirates or the Yankees. And I want you to help me."

The Donora sportswriter laughed at the determination of the boy, but he stopped short. "I'm sure that you'll do all right, Stan. You can count on me."

"Boy, I'd love to get in there and pitch a couple of balls to Waner or that Bill Terry."

"You will," said Johnny Bunardzya. "Just give yourself a little time. Takes a lot of hard work and time to be a big-leaguer."

"I know," said Stan quietly. "But I'm in a hurry."

Stan Musial did move in a hurry, much faster than anyone had anticipated, but not at the very beginning.

In the summer of 1938 he was sent to Williamson of the Mountain States League. He appeared in twenty-six games, won six and lost the same number. In all, he pitched one hundred and ten innings and performed creditably enough. It was a fine showing for a seventeen-year-old high school pitcher. But what was perhaps more important was the fact that even in Williamson they recognized the youngster's ability as a potential slugger. He was called on six times as a pinch hitter and delivered safe base hits each time.

Somehow the Cardinal front office forgot about Stan in the summer of 1939. Musial was still at school and when he got no notice to report to his ball club by June, he began to fret.

"Maybe I'm not as good as some people think," he said to Lillian. "Maybe I'm not as good as I think I am."

Lillian scolded him gently. "You're impatient, Stan. Take your time. The season is young. You'll hear from them soon enough. Don't forget you're still going to high school, and you won't be through for several weeks."

As the days went by and there was no word, Stan really began to worry.

"Maybe I ought to forget about it," he told Lillian. "Maybe I ought to forget about baseball."

"You might try another club," she suggested.

"That's a great idea," snapped Stan, and he followed through.

"I'd like to try out with your club," he said to Pie Traynor of the Pittsburgh Pirates.

"Aren't you signed with the Cardinals?" asked the Pittsburgh pilot.

"Sure," said Stan, "but I think they kind of forgot me."

Pie Traynor smiled wryly.

"Okay, kid. Suppose you work out with the club here. See how you get along. I might be able to find a spot for you."

Stan seemed to get along fine for a while, pitching batting practice for the Pirates' big guns.

"You're in the big time!" said his neighbor Joe Barbao, who managed the local zinc plant ball club.

"Just batting practice," grinned Stan affably.

"Still big time to me," said Joe.

And they both laughed.

But Stan wasn't scheduled for the big leagues just yet. Lillian had been right in the first place. The Cardinals weren't forgetting the young ballplayer, and soon he got the long-awaited orders to report again to the Williamson club.

The year 1939 proved a bigger one for Stan Musial. He pitched in thirteen games, starting and relieving, winning nine against only two losses, striking out eighty-six men. Again, as in 1938, he was called in to pinch-hit, this time more often, and he delivered with even greater authority, collecting a home run, three triples, three doubles—twenty-five hits, giving him a sensational .352 batting average. Williamson captured the league championship on the pitching and batting of the eighteen-year-old kid fresh out of Donora High School.

It was a wonderful season for young Stan Musial. He had personally won nine games with his brilliant pitching, while his big bat won many other games. He was the standout performer of a championship team, and all signs pointed to a better baseball job for the next year. He had chosen baseball as his lifework and he was making good. He knew that he was destined for better things. He felt that he was on his way up.

Lillian needed no convincing either. This was the springtime of their lives and the future looked rosy to both of them.

"Let's get married," said Stan.

"When?" asked Lillian.

"Tomorrow," said Stan.

"But tomorrow's your birthday," protested Lillian.

"I can't think of a better day to get married," persisted Stan.

And so, on his nineteenth birthday Stan and Lillian eloped, and their marriage was one of the brightest days in Donora history. Throngs of well-wishers and friends crowded the comfortable Musial house on Marilda Avenue to congratulate Mama and Papa Musial and the Labash family. It was a happy day for Donora; it was a greater day for Stanley and Lillian Musial.

On November 21, 1939, at the age of nineteen, the young son of a Polish immigrant had won two of life's major victories—he was started on the career of his choice and he was proudly and happily married to the girl he loved.

CHAPTER 7

"Report to the Daytona Beach club in Daytona, Florida."

These were Stan's orders for the spring of 1940, and the nineteen-year-old Musial and his young bride packed their bags and happily headed south. The young couple had good reason for their happiness. The Daytona Beach club was in the Florida State League. It was a long way from the big leagues, but it was a step up from Williamson and the Mountain States League. What the Donora kids didn't know was that the year 1940 was to prove one of the most crucial years in their young lives.

Dick Kerr was managing the Daytona Beach club. Kerr had been star pitcher with the Chicago White Sox in 1919. That was the year the White Sox won the pennant in the junior league, tangled with the Cincinnati Reds in the World Series. It was also the year when the gamblers invaded the White Sox and bribed its key stars to throw the series to the Redlegs. It was the infamous year of the so-called Chicago Black Sox. And in the face of all the bribery and corruption, little Dick Kerr won two games for Chicago, one of them a three-hit shutout. Kerr was a man of great ability and great courage. Fortunately for Stan Musial, as events turned out, Dick Kerr was a man of greater understanding and greater heart.

Stan began to burn up the Florida State League right from the start. With two seasons of minor league baseball under his belt, he was quite confident on the pitching mound and had developed a great deal of baseball know-

how. Now he had the invaluable coaching of manager
Dick Kerr. Stan had the speed to start with. Kerr worked
with him to polish up his curve and his change of pace.

"You're young and strong," said Dick, "but you'll need
more than a fast ball to get into the big leagues. You've
got to develop a really sharp-breaking curve ball. That's
the big pitch. You've got a good fast ball, with plenty of
hop; mix that with a curve and a change of pace and
you've got the makings of a star big-league pitcher.
That's what we have to work on. Let's get going." The
manager and the pitcher went to work with a will. Musial
was the most determined ballplayer on the squad, and he
worked from early in the morning until late at night.

Manager Dick Kerr was at his side constantly, watching, teaching, coaching. "Stan, you're not getting enough
leverage on your pitch. I want you to watch me. See the
way I kick up my leg, bring it down fast? That's where
you waste a lot of speed."

Musial watched and practiced, improving noticeably.
When Kerr had been pitching for the Chicago White Sox
in 1919–1921, he had piled up fifty-three victories and he
knew every aspect of pitching. He saw something in the
big blond youngster that spelled big-league material and
Kerr drove Musial.

When his pitching chores were finished for the day,
Musial practiced batting. He was the first batter in the
batting cage and the last to leave. He loved to swing the
big stick and he thrilled to the feel of a solid base hit.
His untiring efforts paid off. His pitching form became
one smooth and effortless motion. His fast ball fairly
zoomed into the catcher's glove, and under Dick Kerr's
fine leadership, the Daytona team ripped through the
league in easy fashion.

Daytona Beach won the championship of its league in 1940 and young Musial's pitching was the biggest gun in the Daytona Beach defenses. He won eighteen games while losing five. It was the most brilliant pitching performance in the league, and Stan became the star pitcher everybody in the league talked about. It was an amazing performance, even in the Florida State League, for the kid had never put in a full season of professional baseball. In 1940 he was the top pitcher not only of his club but in the entire Florida circuit.

"You're doing great," said Dick Kerr, who had developed a special fondness for Musial and his young wife. "We'll have you up there in the major leagues in no time at all."

At the very beginning of the 1940 season Dick Kerr said, "You've got me puzzled. You've got a big bat. I like the way you hit the ball. I hate to have you just sitting on the bench when you're not pitching. There must be some way we can use your hitting more regularly."

"I used to play in the outfield in Donora, when I wasn't pitching," said young Stan.

"That's it!" exclaimed Dick Kerr. "Get out there in left field. Let's see how you handle yourself. I can use a batter like you out there every day."

Kerr watched his rookie carefully and the more he saw the more he liked him—and the more puzzled he grew.

"Now you're really giving it to me," he said. "You're a natural out there, kid. I just don't know where to use you best. I need your pitching and I need your big bat, too."

Stan smiled, embarrassed by his pilot's open enthusiasm.

"I've never played behind the bat," he said.

"You could play there, too!" insisted Dick Kerr, "but I've got enough of a problem as it is."

"Put me anywhere you want to, Mr. Kerr. I don't really care. Just so long as I can play ball."

Kerr scratched his heead. "We need your kind of pitching." He was thinking out loud. "We can use your kind of hitting." He pulled the cap off his head.

"I tell you what," he said finally. "I'm going to play you regularly in the outfield. I think we can win the pennant with your pitching and batting. I've got a lot of faith in your ability, Stan. I know it will work out just fine."

It worked all right. It worked out so well that Stan played in one hundred and thirteen games that season, and his bat was the deadliest weapon in the entire Daytona Beach offense. He cracked out one hundred twenty-six hits for his club, better than one a game on the average. He hit seventeen doubles, ten triples and scored fifty-five big runs, batting in another big seventy runs for Daytona.

"You're my boy!" Dick Kerr said proudly. "You'll be up there in the big leagues before you know it."

Kerr's optimism was well placed. Stan Musial certainly gave great promise of a brilliant career both on the pitching mound and at the plate. Everything was moving in high gear for the nineteen-year-old from the Monongahela Valley. Then came that unexpected and dramatic break which threatened to cut short a glorious chapter in baseball history.

Stan was playing the outfield that day late in August. Daytona Beach was leading Orlando by a single run. Orlando had men on second and third with their big slugger coming up to the plate.

An infield fly, a pop-up, and there were two out. Still there were men on second and third. A hit would score two runs, give the lead to Orlando and could easily mean the ball game.

The Daytona Beach pitcher had gotten two men out. The next batter drove a low, sinking liner into left field. The batter streaked past first base and headed for second. The men on second and third dashed for home. Out in left field Musial could have played it safe and held the batter to a single, but the two important runs would score easily. He had to get the ball and cut off the winning scores. He raced headlong after the ball, caught it in his glove and turned a complete somersault.

The umpire was on top of the play and saw the ball was still in the outfielder's glove as he completed his full turn. "He's out!" yelled the arbiter.

The side was retired, no runs scored and Daytona Beach held onto its one run margin, but Stan Musial still lay on the ground. He could not get up.

Dick Kerr was at his star ballplayer's side in a flash. "Hurt?" he asked anxiously.

Stan rubbed the bump that had shot up on his left shoulder—his pitching shoulder. "I'll be all right," he said. "I just want to rest a bit. Shoulder hurts, but it will be okay by tomorrow."

He was up on his feet, but he wasn't all right. Still holding the sore shoulder, he walked to the bench and suddenly he remembered the championship basketball game he had played for Donora High. He recalled that desperation basket and the way he had gone crashing into the wall, hurting that same shoulder, that same pitching arm.

"I'm feeling fine," he said to the worried Dick Kerr. "You can pitch me tomorrow, if you want to."

But Dick Kerr knew better, he rushed Stan off to the hospital, where the injury was treated. He was told in no uncertain terms that rest was the only cure.

That injury was not a superficial injury. It was an injury which was going to make Stan Musial completely useless as a pitcher. It was an injury which threatened to cut short Stan Musial's baseball dreams, perhaps send him back to Donora to work in the steel and wire mills for the rest of his life.

CHAPTER 8

Lillian Musial did everything she could for Stan's sore shoulder. She massaged it; she baked it; she used a heating pad. The swelling subsided but the pain persisted.

"You can't pitch tomorrow," said Lillian. "You can't possibly pitch."

"I'm pitching," said Stan, "or we don't eat."

"We don't have to worry about eating, Stan. You've got to rest that arm. You can hurt it again."

"Rest won't do it any good," replied the disconsolate ballplayer, and then he added, "Lil, I think my arm is dead. I'll never be able to pitch again."

For a while they were lost in a silence of complete despair. Stan had made his speech and Lillian could find no words with which to comfort him.

"Sleep on it, Stan," she said finally. "There's always the miracle. Maybe there'll be one for us in the morning."

But there was no miracle that morning or the next. The pain was gone but the arm was stiff.

"What are you going to do, Stan?"

He didn't answer at once. He looked at his young bride and kissed her. "I'm going to try to pitch," he said.

"I'll be praying for you," said Lillian.

Dick Kerr had his doubts. "Why don't you wait a couple of weeks before you get out there on the mound?"

"I'm in a hurry," said Musial. "I want to find out if I've really got a dead arm, or if I'm still a pitcher. I have to know."

He found out soon enough. Orlando clobbered his

pitching all over the park, and Stan was out of the game before he had had a chance even to warm up. He was the most miserable youngster in the world that afternoon as he sat in the clubhouse after the game, watching the other fellows dress, listening to all the small talk and baseball chatter. He was still sitting on his stool, weary and down-hearted, after the last player had left the dressing room, when Dick Kerr found him silent and brooding.

Bighearted Dick Kerr watched him from the door for a while, wondering what he could say to ease the kid's heartache—and there was nothing he could say.

"Aren't you getting dressed?" he muttered at last.

Stan turned around.

"What's that? What did you say?"

"I asked you whether you were going to sleep here."

Stan didn't crack a smile.

"No. Not tonight. I've still got my rent paid."

Dick pulled up a stool, sat down.

"The world hasn't ended, kid."

"Might as well."

"So you won't be a pitcher," put in Kerr. "There are eight other guys on the team."

"They pay me for pitching," was Stan's retort.

"The club pays a lot more for good hitters, and I think you can make the grade as a hitter. But Stan, you've got to be patient. You've got to take time to find out for yourself."

"Maybe I can't hit too good any more, either."

"Can't tell until you try."

Stan was lost in thought for a while.

"I haven't got the time to try," he said quietly.

"You're in an awful big hurry, aren't you?" said Kerr.

"Yeah," countered Stan, smacking his fist into his

glove. "Lillian's going to have a baby. We've got to eat."

Dick Kerr jumped right off his stool, grabbed Musial and hugged him.

"So you're going to be a papa!"

He forgot all about baseball for a minute.

"Great! That's big news, kid! Wait till I tell my missus! Won't she jump! Glad to hear it, kid! Glad to hear it!"

"Thanks," said Stan quietly. "Maybe you know now why I'm feeling this way. I guess it's back to the steel mill in Donora. Can't live off a bad arm and a wish."

"What are you talking about?" demanded Kerr. "Where do you come in with all this going-back-to-the-mill stuff? You're not giving up baseball because you got a bump on your arm, are you? You don't give up that easy! From now on in, you're my regular left fielder on the team. I'll say it again—you can make the grade as a hitter, if you'll take the time. Just you remember that you've got a baby to feed every time you get up to the plate! You'll deliver!"

"Think I can," said Stan, suddenly feeling himself full of fight again. He was looking straight into his manager's eyes. "I'll be in there all the time, swinging. Dick, I've just got to make good now—more than ever."

"That's the spirit!" snapped Kerr. "Now you're talking! See you in the park tomorrow. Batting practice!"

"You bet!"

Dick Kerr walked toward the door.

"Thanks!" shouted a rejuvenated Musial.

"For what?" asked the little manager.

"Dick, thanks for everything. Thanks for believing in me; I'll never forget this."

Kerr was smiling as he opened the door. Then he had a sudden thought, stopped short and came back to Musial who was finally beginning to shed his baseball uniform.

"I've been thinking," said Kerr, after a moment.

"Yeah?" asked Stan, suddenly unsure. Maybe he was in for a let-down after all.

"I've been thinking—with the baby coming, maybe you and Lillian could use a little more room."

"Aw, we'll get along," said Stan, relieved that he wasn't being faced with another baseball problem.

"You know," persisted Dick Kerr, "me and the missus have just got into a bigger house."

"That's what they tell me."

"How about moving in with us?" asked the bighearted manager. "We've got plenty of space. The missus gets lonely. She'd like to hear baby noises around the house and, besides, you don't want to be leaving Lillian alone with a brand-new youngster."

The speech came fast and all at once. Stan wasn't sure he was hearing right. Here was his manager inviting him to live at his house, making it sound as if he and Lillian were going to do him a favor.

"You don't have to tell me right now," said Dick Kerr. "Think about it. Talk to Lillian. You can tell me tomorrow."

And he was gone before Stan could thank him.

Young Musial was making a hundred dollars a month during the six months season. That wasn't very much. It totaled six hundred dollars for the year, less than twelve dollars a week. Dick Kerr was not only encouraging him to stick to the game for what the future might bring; he was also offering him the one way that he and Lillian and the child could get along.

The Musials moved in with the Kerrs, the baby was born there and the wonderful manager of the Dayton

Beach club had helped the youngsters from Donora in their first great crisis in their young married lives.

The first child born to the new Musial family was a big, strapping boy, and both Stan and Lillian agreed on his name, Richard, after one of the really big men in baseball—Richard (Dick) Kerr.

CHAPTER 9

Stan was ordered to report to Columbus, Georgia, the St. Louis Cardinal's farm camp. His impressive eighteen wins for the Daytona Beach club, plus his amazing .311 batting average, had marked him as a likely candidate for one of the better leagues in organized baseball.

"I'll have to tell them about the arm," he told Lillian, before leaving for the training camp.

"Tell them about your batting," urged his young wife.

"Sure," said Stan, and only his great drive and his love for the game were able to beat down somewhat the fears he carried with him to Georgia.

Clay Hopper was manager of the Columbus team. He was hungry for pitchers. The minute Stan showed up at camp, Hopper grabbed him and hustled him into his uniform.

"We can use you here, kid. Maybe you won't win eighteen, but if you can win a dozen that'll suit me, too!"

Stan tried to tell him at once that his arm was dead, that he couldn't pitch any more.

"What are you talking about?" demanded Hopper.

"I hurt my shoulder, can't pitch any more," said Stan. "But I can hit. I hit .311 for Dick Kerr at Daytona, played regularly in left field."

Clay Hopper looked at the youngster, unbelieving.

"It says here in the book that you're a pitcher. You won eighteen for Daytona Beach, didn't you?"

"Yes, sir, but . . ."

Stan didn't get a chance to finish.

"Then get into your uniform and pitch! I'll decide what position you play on this ball club."

Branch Rickey, general manager of the whole St. Louis Cardinal system, was down in Columbus. So was Burt Shotton, who was then his right hand man. Rickey was not around when Stan took his turn on the pitching mound for the first time in a spring training game against the St. Louis Cards, but Shotton was a close and careful observer. What he saw wasn't much.

Stan got by the first two big-league batters without too much trouble, though they hit him hard enough. Terry Moore blasted him for a couple of line drives over the wall and out of the park. Johnny Mize powdered his pitching for a couple of homers.

"I told you I can't pitch any more," said young Musial, disgusted with his own performance.

"You don't have to tell me that again," said Clay Hopper. "How did you ever get those eighteen wins in Daytona? They must be blind down there in Florida. What happened to you, son?"

"My arm wasn't dead then," snapped Stan. "Why don't you see what I can do with my bat?"

"I will," replied Hopper, not overly excited about it. "I will. In the meantime keep pitching. That's what we need —pitching and lots of it."

Burt Shotton watched the Donora kid when Stan finally did get a chance to swing his bat.

"That boy Musial can powder the ball. He's a solid hitter," he said, watching Stan clout the ball like a veteran.

Stan hadn't lost any of his power at the plate. He had become stronger, more determined, and was hitting the ball harder and on a line.

"He came up as a pitcher," said Hopper.

"I watched him pitch," said Shotton.

"Dead arm."

"I know."

"Back to Dayton, I guess," suggested Hopper.

"I don't know. Not the way he's hitting the ball," said Shotton, as he followed the ball over the fence. "We can use that kind of hitting any time."

Burt, who later managed the Brooklyn Dodgers to a National League pennant, called his boss Branch Rickey to watch the Donora youngster.

"He hit .311 for Daytona," he explained, "and he was pitching and playing the outfield regularly. I like the way he hits the ball. Got a smooth, easy, effortless, but powerful, swing, and he's a very determined youngster, I like him."

"Looks good to me," said Rickey. "Springfield can use a hard-hitting outfielder. Get hold of Ollie Vanek. Tell him to forget about the boy's pitching. Use him out in the field. We'll keep an eye on the boy. Maybe we've really got something."

Ollie Vanek, who had known Stan as a pitcher when Ollie managed the Monessen ball club, had watched the Donora boy, too.

"What are we going to do with a dead arm in the outfield?" he complained.

"Did you see him whack the ball all over the field?" asked Shotton.

"Sure! But his arm is dead! How is he going to throw?"

"He'll be all right. Let's try him, a couple of weeks—"

"Maybe," persisted Vanek. "All right, I'll take him. But you've got to promise me the first throwing outfielder that comes along. I got to have an outfielder with a strong throwing arm."

Shotton promised, but he never had to deliver. Once the season got under way in Springfield, Missouri, Ollie Vanek forgot all about that sore arm, and it was Stan Musial's big bat which made him forget it.

Right from the start Stan tore into the pitching of the Western Association with a vengeance and really hammered the ball. The first couple of games Musial slugged out a single, a double, a triple. In the third game of the 1941 season he smashed two doubles and a tremendous home run.

Ollie knew that Stan could hit the ball, but he had never dreamed that he had acquired one of the game's most powerful sluggers for his ball club. And if he had worried about that dead arm, it was still an arm a runner couldn't take any liberties with. The pre-season talk gets around pretty quickly and the entire Western Association had heard about Musial's dead arm long before the first cry of "Play ball!" But Stan dispelled the rumor fast, cutting down runner after runner at third base, whenever the runner thought he could steal an extra base on Musial's weak arm.

"You're my man!" shouted Ollie Vanek in jubilation, as Stan slammed out one slashing drive after another, and sparked Springfield to first place in the league standings.

In eighty-nine games with the Western Association Springfield club, Musial hammered out one hundred and thirty-two hits, twenty-seven doubles, ten triples and twenty-six home runs. He hit three of those home runs in one game for Springfield, and even though he played in only eighty-seven of the one hundred and fifty-seven games of the Western Association schedule, he was home run king of the year for that baseball circuit.

He batted in ninety-four runs in those eighty-seven games, better than a run per game, scored one hundred times himself and ended his days in Springfield with the tremendous batting average of .379. Before the season was half over, Tony Kaufmann, looking for help for his Rochester club, phoned the front office of the Cardinal chain for Stan Musial.

"We need him! We need him badly! And we want him! We can win the championship with Musial. Get him for me."

"You're moving, Stan," said Ollie Vanek to his star. "I don't want to let you go, but Mr. Rickey gives the orders. Besides, I'm glad to see you moving up to a better league. Good luck, kid."

"Thanks," said Musial.

"It's a big step," cautioned Ollie. "Rochester is Triple A ball. It's just one step up from the major leagues and the big time."

"I'll be in their swinging," said Stan.

"Swing hard!" urged Ollie Vanek. "You can make it!"

Stan Musial hardly had time to adjust to his new uniform. In his first time up for the Rochester Red Wings he clouted a mighty blast for a home run. It was another league and the pitching was tougher, but Stan scarcely lost his stride. He cracked out seventy-two hits for the Red Wings, ten doubles, four triples, three homers, for a great batting average of .326 in the fifty-four games he played in the International League. He led his club into the International League Championship play-off series against the front-running Newark Bears.

The St. Louis front office was now watching this

twenty-old youngster with renewed interest. Billy Southworth, managing the Cardinals in one of the closest and
bitterest fights for the National League pennant, was
looking around for whatever reserve material he could
pick up for the last weeks of the race for the flag. He had
heard a good deal of talk about Stan Musial and was
anxious to bring him up with the Cardinals.

"He's burning up the Triple A loop with his clouting,"
he said.

"He murdered them in Springfield," counseled coach
Mike Gonzales. "Musial hit .379 there."

"We could use a bat like his up here," added Coach
Buzzy Wares.

Southworth contacted Branch Rickey. "I want that kid
Musial playing for the Red Wings."

"Tony Kaufmann needs him for the play-offs," countered Rickey. "I can't move him up until Rochester
finishes its schedule and the play-offs."

"I need him up here," argued Southworth. "Give us
the kid's bat and I think I can head off the Dodgers for
the pennant."

"After the International League play-offs," promised
the Cardinal boss, and Billy Southworth couldn't ask for
any more just then.

Newark, the big Yankee farm team, was too much for
Rochester that year, but Southworth read with great anticipation the story of the third game of the play-offs,
the only one the Rochester Red Wings could win.

Hank Borowy was pitching for the Newark Bears and
doing a beautiful job of it. But for once the Red Wings
had a pitcher who could silence the bats of the Bears.
Borowy had only one bad inning and he wouldn't have

had that either, except that Stan Musial was hitting for the Rochester Red Wings.

Hank disposed of the first Red Wing up in the third inning easily enough. Dreisewerd, Rochester pitcher, beat out a hit to second for the first Red Wing hit of the game. Myers was an easy second out. Then up stepped Stan Musial to the plate, with the fans yelling for a hit.

Borowy, always tough in the clutches, pitched carefully and deliberately and the count moved to two strikes and three balls. Borowy rubbed up the ball, looked at the Red Wing pitcher taking his small lead off first, then fired into the plate. It was low and aimed to cut just the edge of the outside corner. But it never got there. With his sharp eyes and his quick reflexes, Musial took a mighty cut at the ball and it sailed on a line into left field, banged up against the fence. Dreisewerd scored and Stan, coming fast, rounded second, went into third and, with Frank Kelleher momentarily fumbling the ball, sailed into home plate with a hook slide—safe!

Musial had delivered again! Rochester had scored twice, and that was all there was to the ball game. There was no more scoring in the game. Stan had taken care of all of it, whacking in a run and coming home himself on a triple and an error.

"He's our man!" said Billy Southworth. "I need him for the Cardinals."

September 15, 1941—the play-offs were all over as far as Rochester was concerned.

September 17, 1941—Stan Musial was playing in the uniform of the St. Louis Cardinals.

It was one of those stories you read about and don't believe—the rags-to-riches story. In the spring of 1941 Stan Musial, just twenty years old, was ready for the ash heap of baseball. His pitching arm was dead and all the glories of a great pitching career were so much dead stuff. And now in the short space of four months he was wearing a big-league uniform. This is the way most stories end, but for Stan Musial it was just the beginning.

CHAPTER 10

"We've met somewhere before," said Terry Moore, shaking young Musial's hand, as he welcomed the rookie into the St. Louis Cardinals' fold.

"Yeah," said Big John Mize, quizzically looking over the newcomer, pumping his hand in his big mitt. "We met somewhere."

"Sure did meet," smiled the Donora kid, recalling uncomfortably the way Moore and Mize had belted his pitching just about five months ago in the Georgia training camp. "Hoped you might forget it," he added, a little nervously.

"No!" exclaimed Terry Moore suddenly. "You're not the kid pitcher from Daytona Beach? The one we socked all over the lot, in Georgia?"

Stan nodded. It was like going through the experience again and he couldn't help feeling embarrassed about it.

Moore looked at Mize.

Mize looked at Moore.

"You're the rookie who's been whaling the tar out of the ball for the Red Wings?"

"I've been hitting a bit," allowed Stan.

"And you're the kid pitcher we looked at in Columbus?"

"Guess I am."

"You can't be both of them. I won't believe it!"

"I guess you'll have to believe it," said Stan, trying to pull out of the uncomfortable position as best he could. "I'm not pitching any more. My arm went dead."

"That figures!" said Johnny Mize, and he laughed, and so did Terry Moore—and the tension was broken.

"He's after your job!" Estel Crabtree yelled to Terry Moore.

"You can have it," snapped Moore, "if you can make it."

"More likely get your job," said Johnny Hopp, another of the top Cardinal outfielders.

"Welcome to it!" responded Crabtree. "If he can bang in the pennant for us!" This was the kind of talk Stan had heard in the Western Association clubhouse, in the International League Rochester clubhouse. The half-kidding, half-serious quips and barbs were no different in the big-league clubhouse. It made the rookie feel more at home.

"He can have my job," said Marty Marion, the brilliant St. Louis shortshop, "if it'll give us the pennant."

"Maybe you'll like to try pitching them again—for us," said Mort Cooper, the ace hurler.

Stan might have been overwhelmed by all these generous offers, but he knew the spirit in which they were made.

"I'll sit it out on the bench, fellows, if you don't mind. Maybe that'll be the best way to win the championship."

"You've got something there," said Gus Mancuso, the big St. Louis catcher. "Maybe you can help with the water bucket. They tell me you used to carry the water for the Zinc plant back in your home town. You're experienced, kid!"

They were laughing again, and Stan laughed right along with them. It was all in the spirit of fun. This was the typical good-natured welcome to a rookie and Stan took the ribbing the way it was intended. It made him feel good. He knew that he was being accepted, that he was one of the ballplayers in a St. Louis uniform, fighting for the National League championship.

The St. Louis Cardinals were fighting desperately for the National League flag, just a game and a half behind the league-leading Brooklyn Dodgers. As he sat in the dugout watching the men in the field, it gave Stan a turn to realize that he had been hurled right into the middle of one of the hottest pennant fights in history. It was hard enough for him to realize that he was now a full-fledged major league ballplayer, and that less than a year ago he had been on the verge of giving up and going back to Donora and the steel and wire mill.

"I can't really understand it yet, Lil," he had said to his wife. "I get to feeling that it's all a dream, that I'll be waking any minute to find myself back in Daytona Beach or maybe Monessen, or back home in a pair of overalls."

"It's real, all right, Stan," Lil had smiled. "You made it, and you're a full fledged big-leaguer!"

Still Stan found it hard to believe as he sat on the bench next to Max Lanier, one of the top pitchers, and Walker Cooper, one of the great catchers.

He watched Estel Crabtree bang the ball out of the park. He watched Marty Marion brilliantly covering second base. He watched Terry Moore, Johnny Mize—the rest of the big fellows—take their cuts at the ball, and he wondered how he could have been so cocky about himself only a couple of years back.

"They're great," he said to himself, "the best," and he speculated on the possibilities of replacing the regular Card outfielders with considerably more respect than he had had when he was a kid fresh out of Donora.

He cheered with the rest of the club as the Cardinals

came from behind to wallop Casey Stengel's Braves to win the first game of the scheduled double-header that September 18th, 1941. But he doubted very much that he would be seeing active duty for some time.

They're in the fight for the pennant, he reasoned. Gosh I wish I could play in one of the games, but each game is too important. Billy Southworth isn't going to take chances on a rookie like me.

He was wrong, of course. Manager Billy Southworth had to take a chance with the rookie. Terry Moore hadn't fully recovered from the concussion he had received only four weeks before. Southworth couldn't risk using him in both games of the twin bill.

"You're playing left field in this second game!" he said, and Stan could feel the butterflies in his stomach. He didn't even bother to correct the announcer when he mispronounced his name over the loud speaker. As a matter of fact, he didn't even hear his name. All he could hear was the loud beating of his heart and the butterflies winging around inside him.

"Okay, kid!" called Crabtree. "Let's go!"

Suddenly there he was in left field, trying to get the feel of the turf under him, knowing for sure that every eye was on him.

"It's just a ball game," he muttered to himself.

But it wasn't just another ball game, and Stan knew it.

He was out on a routine play, the first time he got up to bat, and he trotted back to the dugout as fast and as inconspicuously as he could.

"Give yourself a chance," he was saying. "You can't hit them every time."

He kept his eyes to himself in the dugout. He was worried.

The second time he came up to hit there were two men on base, and the kid felt the pressure was on him.

"Get a good one!" yelled Billy Southworth.

"Yeah," the kid muttered to himself. "I'll get a good one!"

Jim Tobin, one of the toughest pitchers in the league, was pitching for the Braves. Stan knew it. He watched Tobin fidget around on the pitching mound. He kept his eyes on him as he went into his stretch. He watched the pitcher take a look at the two men on base, and his eyes were glued on Tobin as he came to his stop position.

"This is it!" spit Stan, as the ball streaked toward the plate. He stepped into the pitch, swung hard and drove the ball on a line over the first baseman's head into right field, scoring two runs. Musial was perched safely on second base before Frank Demaree, the Braves right fielder, got the ball back to the infield.

"Attaboy!" yelled Billy Southworth.

"Great going," said Estel Crabtree, as he trotted out to his position after the inning was over.

"You're doing all right!" said Terry Moore.

Stan felt good but he was still far from being completely sure of himself as a major leaguer.

He got another hit that afternoon—two for four times at bat—and the two runs he had batted in for St. Louis had won the game, shaving the Dodger lead to just one full game. Stan Musial was off to a great start in his first big-league game, but he had yet to prove his right to stay with the Cardinals, had to make good for Lillian and his family. He was in the major leagues at last, and he meant to stay there.

CHAPTER 11

ROOKIE MUSIAL STARS IN CARDINAL VICTORY

MUSIAL BANGS OUT TWO HITS IN DEBUT

ROOKIE STAN MUSIAL BELTS IN WINNING RUNS

Stan read the sports pages avidly the morning of September 18, 1941.

The twenty-year-old youngster from Rochester lived up to all the advance notices. He stands up at the plate relaxed and easy, like a veteran. He pounded the sharp pitching of Jim Tobin for two solid hits. One of them, a sharp double to the right field wall, coming with two out, scored two runs for St. Louis and won the ball game. If the kid can continue to deliver the way he did yesterday, the Cards have a great chance to cop the pennant.

"If the kid can continue to deliver," repeated Stan to himself, dropping the newspaper.

He suddenly wished he had Lillian with him, and his little son Richard, someone to talk to, someone to distract him from the pressures which kept building on him.

"Sure I'm going to deliver," he said aloud, walking over to the window, looking out on the traffic of the busy St. Louis street.

This was the big city. This was the big leagues. This was Stan Musial's great chance. He wasn't going to lose it.

On the 19th of September Stan played his second big-league game, another tough one. Manny Salvo pitched for the Braves. On a good day he was hard to beat, and in this crucial game he was unbeatable. Only once did the St. Louis club threaten to score. Stan Musial started the bombardment with a two-out single. Mize doubled, sending the rookie to third, but Crabtree flied out to end the game. There was one consolation—Brooklyn lost too— and the Cardinals were still just one precious game behind the Dodgers in the race for the flag.

The mood was not a particularly gay one in the clubhouse that afternoon. With only nine games left to play in the hot pennant battle, and the pressure on them all the time, the ballplayers were in a pretty angry mood despite the Dodger loss. Manager Billy Southworth was nettled and said so.

"Salvo made us look like a lot of minor-leaguers. We aren't going to win any pennants just waving our bats like little boys. This is a pennant fight. We've got to win every game. Do you hear that? Every game."

Stan dressed quietly. He was still a comparative stranger with the club but he wished he could have gotten into the discussion of the game in order to let off a little steam.

"I should have gone all the way home on your hit," he offered tentatively to Johnny Mize.

Johnny Mize looked at the youngster. The veteran was as mad as everyone else in the clubhouse, but the rookie's attempt to find fault with himself softened the big fellow.

"You'd have been a dead pigeon," he said. "They'd have had you out at the plate by a mile!"

"Maybe," hedged Musial.

Johnny Mize pulled on his shoes, turned to the kid again.

"You did all right, Musial," he said. "You did fine. If everybody hit like you did, we'd win them all."

Johnny Mize wasn't exaggerating. The rookie had gotten three hits in his first two major league games, and he was just starting to move. During the next ten days he was going to flash one of the most spectacular streaks of hitting in those last St. Louis games.

On the 19th of September he clubbed the pitching of fireball-hurling Paul Erickson for three of St. Louis' eight hits, two singles and a double, and sparked the Cards to a 3–1 victory over the Chicago Cubs to cut the Dodgers' league lead to half a game. Stan was going strong. His doubts were beginning to disappear. With every game he grew more confident. With every time at bat, with every safe hit, he felt more certain that he was in the big leagues to stay.

The next day Billy Southworth didn't play Musial in right field. St. Louis lost. Brooklyn won two games from Philadelphia, increasing their lead to two full games over the Cardinals.

Restlessly Musial watched the play from the bench. I guess Southworth knows what he's doing, he thought, but he didn't say anything. He wasn't going to pit his baseball knowledge against the know-how of the manager.

However, whatever strategy Southworth had on the 21st of September didn't pay off and he put Stan back in the line-up for the double-header with the Cubs on the 22nd, and Musial promptly rewarded his manager's better judgment.

The rookie came to bat five times in the first game and belted Claude Passeau and Ken Raffensberger for four hits, two singles and two doubles. He did more than that; he stole a base and won the game on a great piece of heads-up ball and spectacular base running.

The score was 4–4 when the Cards came up for the last at-bats in the ninth inning. Gus Mancuso was a routine out, but Musial singled for his fourth hit of the game. Cub second baseman Lou Stringer made a great stop and a great throw to retire Estel Crabtree, but Musial was safe at second. There were two out and Raffensberger passed Crespi to get at Croaker Triplett. It was good strategy and should have paid off as Triplett topped a pitch just to the right of the pitching mound. Clyde McCullough, Stan Hack and Raffensberger all went for the ball, but Raffensberger got it and fired to first, just too late. Triplett was safe and the bases should have been filled. But that wasn't the end of the play. Young Musial, coming into third base, saw quick as a flash that home plate wasn't covered. He rounded third, made a daring dash for home and thundered in over the plate with the fifth and winning run for the St. Louis Cardinals as the more than twenty-six thousand fans rose in the stands to give the rookie a great ovation.

The Cardinals were all out of the dugout, beating the youngster's back, wringing his hands.

"Great base running, kid!"

"That's showing them, Stan!"

"You're all right, Musial!"

"Thanks," was all he could say, and he was the first one to get away from the celebration and into the clubhouse shower.

They were still cheering the rookie when the second game got under way, and the youngster continued to answer the cheers with his bat. Five times in that second game Stan faced a parade of Cub pitchers, and twice he came through with base hits to lead the Cardinals in an easy 7–0 victory. The Dodgers split two games that afternoon and the amazing rookie had sparked his club to within one game again of the lead for the pennant.

There was an open date on the 22nd of September. On the 23rd the Cardinals played at Pittsburgh, just a stone's throw from Musial's home town, and Donora came out in force to greet their boy. Papa Lukasz was there, and Mama, too. Lillian was there, of course, and so was his old baseball coach Mike Duda. Jim Russell was there and the Donora sports writer Johnny Bunardzya and Joe Barbao, manager of the Zinc plant baseball team. They were all out there in Pittsburgh that day, to greet their home town star, and to shower him with the usual gifts of a baseball player's "day."

It was a great turnout, but as often happens in the game, the hero of the day tightened up. In the first game of the double-header Musial couldn't get a hit.

The second game was different, however. Stan shook off the tensions of the celebration and came to life. He got three hits for four times at bat, three of the eight Cardinal hits of the game, and treated the Donora fans to the first Musial big-league home run. There were going to be a lot of home runs for Stan in his long career, but that first home run, with Papa and Mama Musial looking on in Pittsburgh, had special significance. Stan never forgot his joy and happiness on that day. He was a big league star, and his father and mother had watched him on the diamond.

Some of the folks from Donora stayed on to see Stan bat in the first run of the three-run sixth inning to beat the Pittsburgh Pirates again on the next day. Some stayed on to see the last Pittsburgh–St. Louis game of the year and watched Stan bang out two hits in four trips to the bat. By this time the Dodgers, who wouldn't be beaten by the seventh- and eighth-place Braves and Phillies, had clinched the pennant and there was little to write about for the St. Louis sports writers, except Stan Musial, the sensational rookie—and they did.

> Rookie Musial breaks up game with tremendous batting.
> Musial continues to amaze fans with his big bat.
> Stan Musial saved the game with a spectacular catch in the ninth inning. He is as great a fielder as he is a batter, and he is batting at over .400.

Stan continued to hit right through the last game of the season and he wound up with the astounding average of .426. In the twelve games he played for St. Louis at the tail end of the 1941 season, Musial went to bat forty-seven times and drove out twenty hits, four of them doubles, one a home run.

"If we had had Musial earlier, if we'd called him up in July," wrote one sports writer, "we would have sewed up the pennant by August."

It was a promise of what was to come.

The twenty-year-old youngster had certainly had a great year. He had played in three baseball leagues and was batting champion, unofficially, in all three of them. He was top batter in the Western Association with his .379 average for Springfield. He was top batter for Rochester and the International League with .326. No one in the National League topped his sensational average of .426 for St. Louis.

The Cardinals were nosed out of the pennant in 1941 but they had found Stan Musial, and Stan Musial was the ballplayer to spark them to their greatest triumphs in the years to follow.

12

The fans came out in droves to watch Stan Musial in action right from the very beginning of the 1942 season. Every exhibition game during spring training was packed with enthusiastic rooters who came especially to see the youngster who had blasted the ball for St. Louis in the dying days of the old season. And the crowds were quite a tribute to the batting and drawing prowess of the twenty-one-year-old rookie from Donora. Stan should have been mighty happy about it. He wasn't. He was on the spot. "I don't know what's wrong with me," he said to his manager after a hitless day at bat in one of the spring exhibition games. "I don't seem to be able to get started."

"Take it easy," suggested Southworth. "You're trying too hard. Relax—just meet the ball and you'll do fine."

But Stan couldn't take it easy. He could not relax. Southworth took him out of the game and Stan had visions of going back to Rochester, even to Springfield.

Just a flash in the pan, thought Stan unhappily.

But Southworth had too much faith in his rookie to let him go. "That boy has real baseball instinct," he said of Stan. "He'll come through. Too much pressure on the kid. A good rest on the bench will do him a lot of good."

It took a little while. Stan didn't do very much in the early weeks of the 1942 battle for the pennant, but Southworth stuck with him and Musial rewarded his manager with a surge of batting when it counted most.

The rookie finally found his batting eye toward the end

of the first month of the season, and from then on his batting average climbed as he drove the ball at a furious clip and led the Cardinals in a great fight for the National League championship.

As in 1941 the battle for the pennant was a torrid affair, with the Dodgers and the Cardinals neck and neck into the last week of the race. It was a race which was not actually decided until the very last day of the season. And Stan Musial was a sensation with his inspirational team play during the stretch run for the pennant.

The turning point of the entire season was reached in a series with the Pirates on September 22nd. The Cardinals needed a victory over the Pittsburgh team as they were in a virtual deadlock with the Dodgers. In the fifth inning of the seesaw struggle, the Cardinals' Whitey Kurowski singled to center. Marty Marion reached first base on a fielder's choice.

Jimmy Brown reached first on an error. All runners advanced and the bases were loaded. Walker Cooper beat out a hit to deep short. A run was in and the bases were still full when Stan Musial stepped up to the plate. Luke Sewell, pitching for Frankie Frisch's Pirates, was a top-notch pitcher in a tight spot. A pennant was the prize riding on every pitch. He knew he had a big four-run lead over the Cards and meant to hold it. Luke hurled his best pitch to Musial. Stan connected, drove it on a line and out of the park for a grand slam home run. St. Louis scored five times in that inning and they weren't to be headed off. That great win over the Pirates inspired the Cardinals to stay abreast of Durocher's battling Dodgers.

The very next day Stan got three hits—two singles and a double—scoring twice—to lead the Cards to a 4–2 victory over the Cincinnati Reds. The following day Stan repeated, hammering out three hits again—two singles and a double—and scoring once.

The Cardinals piled up one hundred and six victories that season, the highest total in the won column since the Pirates, with Honus Wagner and Babe Adams, won one hundred and ten in 1909. St. Louis needed those one hundred and six wins as the Dodgers finished second with one hundred and four victories—and it was the rookie Stan Musial who spelled the difference for the St. Louis club in 1942.

In his first full year in the major leagues, the twenty-one-year-old outfielder cracked out one hundred and forty-seven hits, thirty-two of them doubles, ten triples, ten home runs. He had battled out of an early season slump to bring his batting average up to .315. He was fourth leading batter in the National League, just .015 points below batting champion Ernest Lombardi. Stan Musial was the rookie of the year. He had been a keystone in the structure of the St. Louis ball club. He had helped bring St. Louis home in front of the National League pack for the first time since 1934. He was to go on to greater glory with the Cardinals in the brilliant World Series against the New York Yankees.

The Yankees, under the leadership of Joe McCarthy, had won six American League pennants in the last seven years. They had won their last five World Series in a row, winning twenty games and losing only four. The New York club had developed an air of invincibility. They had breezed to the American League flag and were expected to defeat a tired St. Louis ball club easily. Joe DiMaggio, Phil Rizzuto, Joe Gordon, Bill Dickey, King Kong Keller, Buddy Hassett and Red Rolfe were among the Yankee big guns, and their pitchers were Red Ruffing, Ernie

Bonham, Spud Chandler and the ace rookie Hank Borowy. They came into the series with all the cockiness of champions, ready to crush the St. Louis Cardinals.

And it looked very much as though they were going to do just that in the first game of the fall baseball classic. Red Ruffing was a complete mystery to the Cards for seven full innings. They got their first hit only after two men were out in the eight. Meanwhile the Yankees had piled up seven runs against the hapless St. Louis club.

In the ninth, however, the Cardinal bats began to explode. Four St. Louis runners scored and the bases were full with two out when Stan Musial came to bat. He hit a terrific smash down the first base line. It was labeled hit all over. But first baseman Buddy Hassett made a desperate grab for the ball, got it in the webbing of his glove, and the ball game was over. The Yanks had won it, but the Cardinals went down to defeat only after a magnificent ninth inning rally that almost wrecked the invincible Yankees.

The Cardinals came back for the second game of the series and immediately jumped off to a two-run lead before they were retired in the first inning. They scored a third run in the seventh and it looked like the Cards were turning the tables on the Yanks, with Johnny Beazley pitching shutout ball all the way.

The New York club, however, came to life in the eighth and thirty-four thousand fans in Sportsman Park sat stunned as the Yankee bats swung into action. Roy Cullenbine singled and stole second. DiMaggio singled Cullenbine home and Charlie Keller drove out a two-run homer, knotting the score at 3–3. The old legend of Yankee invincibility began to show again and it seemed like only a matter of moments before the New Yorkers would romp off with the game and the series.

"You can't beat them."

"They've got too much power."

"They're too good."

But the Cardinals were not licked. Enos Slaughter doubled in the St. Louis eighth and the thirty-four thousand fans began to take heart. He took third as Rizzuto dropped Cullenbine's throw and the fans set up a holler. Stan Musial came up to bat and the noise in the stadium began to swell.

"We want a hit!"

"Send him home, Stan!"

"Hit it, Musial!"

Bonham, still pitching for the Yankees, poured the ball over the plate and Stan Musial swung, hit the ball sharply over second base and into center field for a clean single. Slaughter scored with the winning run and the thirty-four thousand fans in Sportsman Park stood and cheered rookie Stan Musial for fully five minutes. It was a great and spontaneous ovation. They were still cheering him as the Yanks went down in the ninth inning. Musial, the spark of the St. Louis team, had won the game for the Cardinals. It was the first World Series win for the Cardinals since 1934. That win, that Musial hit, was to prove the turning point in the 1942 World Series.

The Cardinals traveled to New York and the Yankee Stadium for the third game of the series and banged out a 2–0 victory over the American-Leaguers, Ernie White pitching a six-hit shutout. Stan got one of the five St. Louis hits, as more than sixty-nine thousand fans saw the Yanks blanked in a World Series game for the first time in sixteen years.

Almost seventy thousand fans, a new record of attendance, came to see the fourth game, and the cheering started off with almost the first crack of the bat, as Red Rolfe doubled and Roy Cullenbine singled to get the Yankees off to a 1–0 lead. In the fourth inning, however, a strange silence came over Yankee Stadium as the Cardinals attacked Hank Borowy.

Stan Musial crossed the Yankee defense by beating out a surprise bunt for a safe hit. Walker Cooper singled and went to second as Stan raced into third, daring and beating Joe DiMaggio's bullet throw to third base. Johnny Hopp walked, filling the bases. Whitey Kurowski, crossing up the Yankee strategy again, singled, scoring Musial and Cooper. Marty Marion was walked to get at pitcher Mort Cooper and again the Yanks were crossed up, as Cooper singled home two more runs.

Atley Donald came in to pitch for the Yankees. It was against Donald that Stan Musial came up for the second time in the inning, and he showed no favoritism. He smacked a hit off the Yank relief pitcher, too, a double, scoring Mort Cooper for the sixth run of the Cardinal big inning. And it was a record, too, for the Cardinal rookie as he tied the mark for the most hits in a single World Series game. No one has ever gotten more than two hits in a single inning of a World Series game.

The fans applauded the youngster with mixed feelings. He was on a rival team, but his sensational play had the fans of both teams in a constant uproar of applause. They cheered Musial even as the Yanks went down for their third loss against only one victory in the series.

There were sixty-nine thousand in the stadium for the fifth game of the classic. The fan never gives up on his ball club. But the Yanks were beaten. This time John

Beazley whipped them 4–2. The legend of the invincibility of the Yankees was destroyed, and a happy St. Louis Cardinal club headed home, the new World Champions.

It had been a full year, an unforgettable year for the rookie Stan Musial and he was a tired but happy boy going back to Donora.

"What are your plans, Stan?"

"What are you going to do now?"

The reporters wanted to know. The season was over but the fans were still hungry for baseball news. They were especially hungry for news about the younger stars.

"They want to know something about your personal life," said the sports writers. "They want to know something about your hobbies."

Stan grinned.

"I'm a family man," he said. "I've got a two-year-old son back home. When you've got a two-year-old youngster, he's all the hobby you've got time for."

He smiled and boarded the train for home. The 1942 season was closed on a note of personal victory. But there were bigger years ahead, and 1943 was to prove one of the biggest.

CHAPTER 13

That second year in big-league baseball has always been especially dif-
ficult for the young ballplayer. No matter how great a
year he has had as a freshman major-leaguer, time after
time that sophomore year proves to be a hurdle he can't
climb. Ballplayers call it the sophomore jinx, but if Stan
Musial had ever heard of it, he didn't let on. On the
contrary, from the very beginning of the 1943 training
grind in the Cardinal spring camp at Cairo, Illinois, he
began to powder the ball all over the diamond, and Billy
Southworth, manager of the Redbirds, smiled with con-
siderable gratification, predicting another great year for
his prize rookie.

"He's the coolest young ballplayer I've ever seen," said
the Cardinal pilot. "He's got just one idea in his head
when he gets up there with the bat. He's going to whale
the tar out of the ball, and he does."

The sensational young ballplayer was still only a kid,
as far as big-leaguers were concerned. He was only
twenty-two at the beginning of the 1943 season. But he
approached the plate with the know-how of a veteran
and he hammered the ball like a seasoned star.

In 1942 young Musial had taken some time to get into
his batting stride. In 1943 he assaulted the opposition
with the first cry of "Play ball!" By the middle of May he
was the most feared batsman in the National League.

The season wasn't a month old before the St. Louis
star was in the middle of a big hitting streak. On the
22nd of May Stan lit into New York Giant pitching for

five hits to spark the Cardinals to a twin victory. On the 24th of May Stan drove out four hits against the luckless New York club to win two more games for the St. Louis aggregation. There was no stopping the Redbird slugger and the Cardinals surged into a quick lead in the 1943 pennant race, with young Musial leading the way with a twenty-two consecutive game hitting streak.

Johnson, of the Philadelphia Phillies, put a temporary halt to the rookie's belting at the end of the first week in June, but it was only a five-inning game, and only a very short pause in the sensational record Musial built for himself that year.

For a while the 1943 season was a repetition of 1941 and 1942 schedules, with the Brooklyn Dodgers and the St. Louis Cardinals in a nip-and-tuck battle for the flag. But Stan's bat soon changed the script.

On July 23rd, against those same Giants, Stan went up against five different pitchers. No one could stop him. Cliff Melton was the first New York hurler to face the St. Louis slugger and Stan clipped him for a sharp two-base hit. Bill Sayles was the second Giant pitcher and Stan smashed him for a single. Mel Ott, the Giants' manager, was having his troubles that day. He sent in Harry Feldman against Musial for his third trip to the plate and Musial walloped the best pitch for a tremendous triple. Van Mungo was the fourth New York pitcher and Stan greeted him with his fourth hit of the game. The last of the parade of Giant pitchers was Hugh East and Musial came through with another double to give him five hits in five at-bats.

Mel Ott, one of the greatest all-time hitters in baseball, just watched in utter amazement.

"How do you stop the kid?"

There was no stopping him. He was just reaching his peak. He collected two singles, two doubles and a triple for his afternoon's work, adding insult to injury by stealing a base as well, just to show them he could do something else besides slug the ball.

Toward the end of August, inspired by Musial's hitting, the Cards tore the league apart, winning fifteen straight ball games and completely dominating the league. Billy Southworth had a great ball club, but Stan Musial was the big gun.

On the 23rd of August Musial hammered out two hits for five times at bat to give St. Louis its first game of the double-header against the Boston Braves. In the second game of the afternoon Stan batted out two hits for four trips to the plate to give the Cardinals two victories for the day.

The very next day Stan started the ball rolling for the Cardinals' thirteenth straight by hammering a triple off Manny Salvo in the very first inning. On the 25th, he kept that winning streak alive with one swing of his mighty bat.

Mort Cooper and Al Janey had tied themselves up in a brilliant pitching duel. Both pitchers had hurled shutout ball. It was 0–0 going into the ninth inning and neither side was able to score. In the tenth inning the brilliant Mort Cooper continued his whitewashing of the Boston Braves. Then the Cardinals came to bat and Stan Musial brought a halt to the shenanigans. Harry Walker singled for the Redbirds and up stepped Stan.

"Hit it, Musial!"

"We want a hit!"

"Smack it out of here!" yelled the fans.

Musial responded and hammered the ball to the right

field fence for a three-base hit, scoring Walker with the winning run.

Stan himself was the show. Even when the Cards lost an occasional ball game, the youngster starred. The Redbirds lost the first game of a double-header at the end of August to the Pittsburgh Pirates, but it hadn't been the fault of Musial. All he did in that game was to wallop out three hits in five trips to the plate. He made sure of the second game by collecting another two hits, one of them a double, and hammered in two St. Louis runs to insure the club its victory. Musial wasn't just a show in himself; he was the man who led his club to its second straight pennant. Not since 1922 had any National League team been able to accomplish that feat, but Stan had spelled the difference.

The Cardinals won that pennant by eighteen games. For the second year in a row, they had hammered out more than one hundred victories. They had won one hundred and six games in 1942. In 1943 they won one hundred and five, for a grand total of two hundred and eleven games won in two years. This was the greatest total number of victories for consecutive seasons in the National League since Frankie Chance's Chicago Cubs won two hundred and twenty-three in the 1906–1907 seasons. And Stan was the ballplayer whose bat had sparked those records.

Musial averaged a hit a game in the World Series which followed, but the Yankees were too much for the St. Louis Cardinals in the 1943 classic. Thoroughly aroused by the upset of the 1942 World Championship series, the New York aggregation romped over the St. Louis club, four victories to one defeat. It was too much to expect the Yanks to lose two series in a row.

Stan, like everyone else in the Cardinal's ranks, was sorely disappointed by their poor showing in the championship fight, but he had much to comfort him. The year 1943 had been a great one.

He had played in every scheduled game of the season, plus three more because of tied-up ball games. He had gone to bat six hundred and seventeen times and clouted out two hundred and twenty hits, more hits by far than any other major-leaguer playing in 1943. And of those two hundred and twenty hits, forty-eight were doubles. He led his league in this department, too. He led the league in triples with twenty. He banged out thirteen home runs, scoring one hundred and eight times. He was the batting champion of his league with the sensational batting average of .357. He was the slugging champion of the National League with an almost unbelievable average of .562. He had been up at bat and hit for the tremendous total of three hundred and forty-seven bases. In 1942 he had been the rookie of the year. In 1943 he was easily the most valuable player of the year. And that is exactly how the Baseball Writers' Association felt about it.

Thirteen out of twenty-four writers voted him first place in the annual national poll to select the outstanding player of the year. Catcher Walker Cooper of the Redbirds was his closest rival, with five first-place votes. Stan was the only man to be named on every one of the writers' ten-name ballot. He soared away with the honors, amassing two hundred and sixty-seven points to one hundred and ninety-two for his teammate. It was a great testimonial to a great player, the youngster who had overcome the nightmare of an injured arm, which had threatened his career, and in two short years had won himself the two top honors of the national game.

In the fall of 1943 Stan Musial, the rookie of the year of 1942, the most valuable player of the year 1943, returned home to Donora, to his family and his friends and the mills, a hero, baseball's newest and brightest star.

14

Musial started the 1944 baseball season right from where he had left off in 1943. His bat bludgeoned out the base hits for the St. Louis Cardinals and the Redbirds were off and running, aiming high for a third straight pennant in the National League. Every time the six-foot, one hundred and seventy-five-pound batsman came up to the plate he spelled trouble for the opposition and the Cardinals all but swept the rest of the clubs out of the league.

Max Lanier, who pitched the lone win for the St. Louis club in the 1943 World Series, hooked up with Preacher Roe of the Pittsburgh Pirates in the opening day game, and both pitchers were outstanding. For the first five innings they matched their pitching wizardry and neither club could score,

In the St. Louis sixth inning, Roe walked Max Lanier. Emil Verban forced Lanier at second. The reliable Johnny Hopp doubled, sending Verban to third, and Stan Musial stepped up to the plate. With first base open, the strategy called for walking the St. Louis slugger, but Roe was pitching sharply and the Pittsburgh manager gambled.

"Don't give him anything good to hit at," he ordered. "Make him go after the bad one."

That was the first mistake of managerial brainwork of the afternoon. It cost the Pirates the game.

Stan looked at a couple of bad pitches. Roe looked to his pilot for a signal, the signal to put Stan on, but the signal wasn't coming.

The Pirate hurler came to his stop position, twisted a curve just off the plate, but not off far enough, and Stan stepped into it and whistled the ball over second base for a clean hit, breaking the scoreless deadlock and sending Verban home with the first St. Louis run of the brand new season.

Roe knew that it had been an error to pitch to Musial, but a manager's orders are orders, and they have to be followed. He proved how wrong his pilot was by disposing of the next two Cardinal batters, but by that time it was too late. St. Louis' one run was enough to win its opening game, as Lanier, pitching brilliantly, shut the Pirates out with just two hits.

The Cards, however, got themselves another tally for insurance, and it was Stan again who got it for them.

The twenty-three-year-old star led off the eighth inning with another single, his second hit of the day, stole second, then on a great run and a beautifully executed slide, he came home with the second and last St. Louis run of the game on a single by Whitey Kurowski.

In the second game of the young season, St. Louis topped the Pirates again, 5–3, with Stan getting his usual hit and run. In the third game Musial varied the routine by hammering Paul Derringer for a couple of hits in three trips to the plate, scoring a run as the Cards blanked the Chicago Cubs 4–0.

On their fourth outing of the schedule, Stan got himself two for four, batted in a couple of runs and scored one on his own. In their fifth battle Stan walloped a double and a single, again two for four, as St. Louis got off to a running start for the National League flag with a streak of five straight wins. From the very beginning it looked like neither the Cardinals nor Stan Musial could be stopped.

The Cincinnati Reds finally stopped St. Louis in the sixth game of the 1944 season, but Stan kept rolling, smacking out a sharp single to keep his personal hitting streak alive. By the end of June St. Louis was leading the National League pack by eight full games, and Stan Musial had banged out ninety-two hits in two hundred and forty-three times at bat, driven in forty runs and scored fifty-one himself. By July 1st the Cards had amassed forty-three victories against only nineteen defeats, and it was Stan's tremendous hitting at the fantastic clip of .379 that was outdistancing the opposition.

St. Louis took undisputed possession of first place in the league standings on April 30th. That was the day Stan doubled and singled in four times at bat to send his club to a 4–2 victory over the Chicago Cubs. And from the end of April, through the rest of the season, there was no heading off the victorious parade of the Redbirds.

On September 22, 1944, the Cardinals clinched their third straight National League pennant, as Musial hammered out two hits for five turns at bat, whipping the Boston Braves in the tenth inning of a grueling game, 6–5. And to celebrate their league championship, in the second game of the double-header of the afternoon, Stan followed up with a ringing two-run homer to beat Jim Tobin and the Braves by the score of 6–5.

It was another great year for the young fellow from Donora. He led his league in most-base-hits for the year with a grand total of one hundred and ninety-seven. He was the leading two-base hitter with fifty-one doubles for the season. Stan lost the 1944 batting crown to the

Brooklyn Dodgers' Dixie Walker by just ten points. Stan battled Dixie for the coveted batting title, coming in with a brilliant .347 batting average for his third season in the major leagues and copping again, for the second straight time, the slugging championship of the league with a total of three hundred and twelve bases for five hundred and sixty-eight times at bat and a spectacular .549 slugging average. Stan was still the biggest batting gun in the senior baseball circuit.

He carried that big gun into his third World Series in three straight years. This time, however, there was a slight change in the cast. The invincible Yankees had been beaten at last and it was the surprising St. Louis Browns who took the American League championship to meet Billy Southworth's club in the fall classic.

Billy Southworth, incidentally, was the first National League manager since John McGraw in 1921–1924 to lead a club to three straight pennants. He had done it by piloting the Cards to one hundred and five victories, setting a new record for the National League. The St. Louis Redbirds were the first club in the senior circuit to win more than one hundred games in three straight seasons. Records have a way of forecasting coming events and baseball fans all over the country expected Billy Southworth's charges to ride roughshod over the Browns, who won their pennant on the last day of the season with a 5–2 victory over the Yankees. The fans were in for a bit of a surprise.

It was the St. Louis Browns who got off winging, beating Mort Cooper and the Redbirds in the opening game of the series on only two hits. Gene Moore singled for the American-Leaguers in the fourth inning and George McQuinn hammered in two runs with a smashing home run. Those were all the hits and runs Mort Cooper allowed, but they were enough, as Denny Galehouse scattered seven blows to limit the Cardinals to a lone tally. In this game Stan banged a single off Galehouse in three trips to the plate, but not even Marty Marion's two doubles could set the Cards moving.

In the second game, Nelson Potter and George Muncrief limited the St. Louis slugger Musial to a lone single in five times at bat, and the Cards barely beat the Brownies in the eleventh inning, 3–2. The series stood even at 1–1, but everyone knew that this classic was no runaway for the St. Louis National-Leaguers.

Jack Kramer of the Browns made the baseball world really sit up and take notice in the third game for the championship, limiting Musial to a long single and the Cards to two runs, as the American-Leaguers romped off with the game, 6–2.

The National-Leaguers had a clubhouse meeting. Manager Southworth took personal charge of the meeting.

"What's the matter with you guys? You took one hundred and five games in the pennant race and you're letting the American-Leaguers walk all over you! I want you all out for batting practice in the morning! You can't win games without hitting the ball! Now let's get out on that field and play like big-leaguers!"

The Cards banged the ball around in batting drill. They finally got to banging the ball around in the game, too. As usual, it was Stan Musial who got the Redbirds off and running.

In the very first inning of the fourth game of the series, Johnny Hopp singled and Stan followed with a terrific home run drive over the right field roof. St. Louis was ahead, 2–0, and they weren't to be headed, as Stan hammered out two more hits, a double and a single, to spark the Cards to a 5–1 win. The classic was tied for a second time, each club with two victories and two defeats.

The Brownies went all out to go in front again in the fifth game and Denny Galehouse almost did it again, limiting the Cards to six hits. But this time Dame Fortune smiled on Mort Cooper and it was a couple of Redbird homers which brought home the victory to the National-Leaguers.

The win put the Cards on top for the first time in the 1944 series, and in the sixth game, with Max Lanier and Ted Wilks sharing the pitching duties, they went on to a 3–1 victory over the Browns—and the World Championship, their second in two years.

For Stan, it was his best series in three years of championship play. He had gotten seven hits for twenty-three times at bat for a good average of .304. He had blasted out two doubles and his first home run in the fall classic. He could look to the year 1944 as another great year of baseball. But with his glove and his bat put away for the season, Stan prepared to serve his country in its armed forces.

He went home to Donora after the 1944 baseball season. Then, January 23, 1945, the great National League slugger swapped his baseball uniform for the blue uniform of a sailor.

Behind him, in Donora, were his wife Lillian, his son Richard, who was now three years old, and his daughter Geraldine, just six weeks.

It isn't easy leaving loved ones behind, but Stan was not alone. Fathers all over America were leaving loved ones at home in order to take part in America's great struggle for liberty. And baseball sent its greatest stars to join in the greater conflict. Terry Moore, Enos Slaughter, Hank Bauer, Joe DiMaggio, Bob Feller, Bill Dickey, Red Ruffing, Phil Rizzuto, Hank Greenberg, Johnny Mize, Bobby Brown, Mickey Harris, Mickey Cochrane, Ted Williams and many more answered the roll call for Uncle Sam, and served him well. Stan Musial, reporting for duty, expected to do no less for his country.

CHAPTER 15

Stan Musial served for fourteen months as a navy man in 1945–1946, stationed for the most part in that key defensive spot in the Pacific, Pearl Harbor. It was in 1945 that the vainglory of the notorious Axis powers came tumbling down on their heads as the United Nations brought Tojo, Mussolini and Hitler to their knees in unconditional surrender. At the beginning of March, 1946, Stan Musial was discharged from the United States Navy to return to his home in Donora, Pennsylvania, and then back to the more peaceful wars of the baseball diamond.

Actually, however, the world of baseball was not exactually a peaceful sphere in 1946, and its wars were severely complicated by a foreign aggression. A gentleman by the name of Jorge Pasquel, hailing from Mexico, was suddenly imbued with the possibilities of big-league baseball below the Rio Grande. Baseball has always been a popular game with our Latin American friends and neighbors, and they play the game not only in the spring and summer but in the fall and winter as well. Baseball is a year-round sport in the warmer climate of the Caribbean, and Mexico and Señor Pasquel's idea was to raid the National and American League's star players. Pasquel was a multimillionaire, and he offered tremendous salaries to the outstanding players of both leagues. This was enough to start a battle royal. It certainly created a great deal of excitement among the players and near panic in the front offices of every big-league club. It caused consternation for the St. Louis Cardinals. Jorge

Pasquel was making overtures to their star slugger Stan
Musial, even before he had had time to get back into a
Cardinal uniform.

Stan was just back from his tour of duty in the Navy.
He was back home with his family enjoying every minute. One afternoon the doorbell rang. Stan opened the
door to greet a stranger. He was an impressive-looking
man, imposingly dressed.

"I'm Jorge Pasquel."

"Come in."

Stan had already heard of the gentleman. Mickey
Owen, the great young St. Louis catcher, had already
signed up with the Mexican League. Max Lanier, St.
Louis' ace pitcher, had also signed up with Pasquel. So
had Sal Maglie, Freddie Martin, Lou Klein and a host of
others.

"I'll come to the point fast," said Jorge Pasquel.

He took a wad of bills out of his pocket and slapped
them on the table.

"There's seventy-five thousand dollars there," he said.

Stan couldn't help being impressed by the size of the
bait. He waited for details.

"Mr. Musial," said Pasquel, "I want you to play with
our new league. You're a big star. You're the man I want.
That's just a bonus," continued the Mexican entrepre-
neur, "for signing with my league."

Young Musial, just out of the Navy, was fascinated.
"That's a big chunk of money," he said.

It certainly was a big chunk of currency, considering
that Stan's contract with St. Louis for 1944, the year after
he had been voted the Most Valuable Player in the National League for 1943, was a mere fifteen thousand dollars. Sam Breadon, owner of the Cardinal baseball chain,

was never one to overpay his players. On the contrary, the Card stars were the lowest-paid baseball players in the game. That seventy-five thousand dollar bonus Pasquel was offering was a tremendous bait. But that wasn't all Señor Pasquel was offering.

"It's all yours," he said, "if you sign this little contract." He slapped the contract on the table, too.

"Five years," he continued, "at thirty thousand dollars a year."

Stan did some quick figuring.

"That makes it two hundred twenty-five thousand for the run of the contract," he said.

"Right!" declared Pasquel. "Sign!" and he pressed the fountain pen into Musial's hand.

"Not so fast," Stan said. "Not so fast."

But that seventy-five thousand dollars cash held him. He'd have to play top baseball for five years for Sam Breadon to collect that much money. He would have to win the batting championship for five years running— or come close to it—to draw that kind of a contract from the St. Louis club.

Maybe the Navy took something out of my bat, thought Stan. Maybe I won't be able to hit them the way I did before I went into the service. What will Sam Breadon pay me then?

He said nothing but Pasquel, sensing his indecision, decided not to force the issue.

"Suppose you think about it," he suggested, fingering the roll of bills.

"I'll think about it," said Stan.

"We're building a top-notch league in my country," added Señor Pasquel. "Sal Maglie, Max Lanier, Mickey Owen. We'll get Terry Moore and Enos Slaughter. You'll have good company. I'll get the best players, the greatest stars in baseball at your side."

"Sure," agreed Stan, but he wasn't too sure. "Just give me a couple of days to think about it.

"Of course," consented Pasquel, returning the contract to his pocket. "Shall I leave this seventy-five thousand dollars as a binder?"

Stan thought a moment.

"Better take it with you," he said finally.

"Anything you say."

Pasquel returned the money to his billfold.

"Seventy-five thousand dollar bonus," he repeated. "Thirty thousand dollars a year for five years. You'll make no mistake. I'll make you the biggest star in all of baseball. You'll be the ideal of all my people, and the wealthiest."

"Thank you," said Stan, and he walked the enterprising Mexican to the door and closed it behind him.

"That's a lot of money," said young Musial to himself, once he was alone. "Why don't I take it?"

"Take what?"

Stan looked up to see his wife Lillian standing in the living room, his one-year-old Geraldine in her arms.

"Take what, Stan?" she repeated.

Stan tried to pull himself together.

"Sit down," he said. "We've got something to think about."

Lil listened to the whole story, the details on the Pasquel venture, the players who had jumped to the Mexican League, the offer he had just been made.

"What do you say, Lil?" he asked.

"Quite an offer," answered Lil. "We could live on that kind of money. We could live wonderfully for the rest of our lives and never have to worry about the future."

"I guess that's so," said Stan.

"Then what's bothering you?" questioned his discerning young wife.

"We'd have to move out of Donora. We'd have to move to Mexico. You, Richard, Geraldine."

"I've been thinking of that, too."

"Would you like it? Could we have all of our wonderful friends and relatives?"

"Whatever you say, Stan. You make the decision."

"It's not easy," offered her husband.

"I know," said Lil.

They were both quiet for a moment.

"Whatever you decide," said Lil finally, "will be all right with us. You've always done the right thing, Stan. It's up to you."

It was a difficult decision for the young ballplayer to make.

"Sam Breadon isn't paying you what you ought to be getting. A man who wins the Most Valuable Player Award, the man who leads the league in batting and slugging, the man who is the spark in three straight pennant years and two World Championships deserves a better contract from the Cardinal office. Look at the money some of the other big boys are getting on the other clubs. Sam Breadon will never pay you the way he ought to."

That was the kind of talk Stan Musial heard about him.

"But the St. Louis club gave me my chance," argued Stan. "They didn't drop me when my arm went bad in Daytona Beach. They gave me the breaks. How can you turn on a club like that?"

"You can give your family everything it needs and

wants with the money Pasquel is offering you," said the slugger's well-meaning friends.

"I'd have to take my family out of the United States," countered Musial. "I'd have to bring up my children in another country."

Stan weighed all the arguments and finally made up his mind.

"I want to thank you for everything you've done for me, Mr. Breadon," he said to the owner of the St. Louis Cardinals. "I appreciate everything you've done, but this Mr. Pasquel is making me a mighty fine offer."

"You're not going to take it?" thundered Sam Breadon, who had already lost three men to the Mexican League.

"I'm afraid I have to take it," said Stan.

Sam Breadon burned up the wires. He got his new manager Eddie Dyer on the phone.

"You've got to stop him, Eddie! You can't let him go! He'll be in the park tonight. His last game for us, he told me. Talk to him. Do something! We don't want Musial to skip to that Mexican League! If we lose Musial, we lose the championship."

"Can I offer him something?" asked the calmer Eddie Dyer. "Can I offer him a new contract?"

"No!" bellowed Sam Breadon. "But do anything else! Do something! We need that kid in St. Louis!"

"Okay," said Eddie quietly. "I'll do my best."

He hung up the phone, shrugged his shoulders. How was he going to be able to talk Stan out of a two hundred twenty-five thousand dollar contract? What did he have to offer?

Dyer was down to the park early that night. He waited for Stan to show up. He tried to figure some new approach with a special gimmick, a gimmick to counteract the lure of the thoroughly inviting contract the Mexicans were offering his star slugger. Eddie was a smart manager and he knew his baseball players. He had held practically every position in the big baseball farm system of the St. Louis Cardinals and no one had had more experience with the way baseball players think and act. For once, however, he was stymied. He just didn't know how he was going to approach Stan Musial.

"Hi?" he said, casually, when the big fellow walked into the clubhouse.

"Hi," said Stan. He was in no mood for conversation. He had made up his mind to take Pasquel's offer and play for the Mexican League, but he couldn't say he was very happy about it. He had been happy as a Cardinal, and had developed into one of the great stars in baseball under Cardinal managers. Now that he made up his mind he wanted to leave as quickly and quietly as possible. He kept on walking but Dyer stopped him.

"Where are you going?"

"To get into my uniform."

"What for?"

"We're playing tonight, aren't we?"

"Shouldn't make much difference to you."

The two men looked at each other. Stan knew that Dyer wasn't just needling him. Dyer knew he had touched a soft spot in Musial's armor.

"What's the matter?" challenged Stan. "Don't you want me to play for you?"

"I'd like you to play every game of the season for us," countered Dyer. "You know that we need you. You belong here, Stan." He paused as Musial looked away. "Mr. Breadon just had me on the phone," continued Eddie. "I hear you've signed with the Mexican League."

"Not yet."

"Oh!" said Eddie.

"But I'm going to," added Stan quickly.

There was another silence—Stan embarrassed and Eddie stalling for time.

Dyer wracked his brain. He had to convince Musial that he was wrong. "I can't say that I blame you," said the St. Louis manager at last. "I'd like to be making that kind of money myself."

"If Mr. Breadon made me an offer like that—" began Stan angrily. He didn't finish his statement.

"But Mr. Breadon won't make you any offer," Dyer continued, "and there are other things besides money."

"Sure," agreed Musial. "Sure there are other things, but a man ought to be paid what he's worth."

Eddie took the cap off his head, wiped the perspiration from his forehead.

"I know," he said. "You're not getting what you ought to get, but you signed the contract, Stan."

"That's right."

"You sign a contract and that's just as good as giving your word," continued Eddie Dyer.

Stan had nothing to say. The manager had hit a bullseye.

"You've got to break the contract to jump to the Mexican League," Dyer went on. "A man doesn't break a contract. A man doesn't go back on his word. It isn't honorable."

Musial was still silent. He could think of many things to say but he was too hurt to say anything.

"You wouldn't want your kids to think you broke your word. You wouldn't want them to think their father isn't an honorable man?"

This time Eddie waited for Stan to speak, and Musial studied the face of his new manager. It was an honest, sincere face.

"Guess not," he said at last. "No, I wouldn't have them thinking that of me. I guess that's the big thing with all of us people. I gave my word to Mr. Breadon. I can't break my word."

"Well, then?" said Eddie, asking for the clincher.

It was Stan's turn to take off his hat, dry his forehead.

"You're right," he said at last. "You can count on my playing in every game. I'm not going to Mexico."

It was a tough decision, but Stan made it. There was a letter, forwarded to Sam Breadon, in which Stan was reported to have asked Pasquel to forward that promised seventy-five thousand dollar bonus, that Musial had reconsidered and would report to Mexico on August 1st. It caused another momentary flurry in the St. Louis offices and made for a lot of newspaper publicity. Actually, the letter was a forgery, the work of a crank. Stan had made his final choice in the clubhouse the night of his talk with Eddie Dyer. He was not to regret it, and the year 1946 was to prove one of the most dramatic years in the baseball history of the St. Louis Cardinal star, Stan Musial.

CHAPTER 16

With World War II coming to a successful conclusion, baseball's greatest stars were released from service and returned to the diamond. Enos Slaughter, Walker Cooper, Howie Pollet, Alpha Brazle, Danny Litwhiler, Murray Dickson, Johnny Beazley, Freddie Martin and, of course, Stan Musial were back in the big Cardinal line-up. Pete Reiser, Peewee Reese, Gene Hermanski, Carl Furillo, Billy Herman, Cookie Lavagetto were among the Brooklyn stalwarts who returned to the Dodger fold. And the two outstanding teams resumed their perennial battle for the National League flag.

The 1946 race for the pennant was to prove the greatest in National League history. From the very start of the season to the last scheduled game, baseball fever ran high. The two magnificent clubs went at it hammer and tongs, with first one club, then the other, taking the lead in the pennant drive. Brooklyn, however, put on a spurt toward the end of May, and ten days later took a commanding lead of four and one-half games over the second place Cardinals. On July 11th St. Louis came into New York to play against the Giants, always a tough club for the Cards, and to try to close the gap between the Dodgers and themselves in the race for the flag. Right in the middle of that great battle was the brilliant Stan Musial.

Eddie Dyer, in his freshman year as manager of the Cards, had one of the top squads in baseball. There was one weakness in the club, however. Eddie needed a good

104

first baseman. He experimented for a while using a couple of men at the bag—including Dick Sisler, son of Hall of Fame George Sisler—but the results were not good. A weak spot at first base could cost the team a pennant. He worried himself sick about the problem, then abruptly made up his mind.

"I want you on first base," he said to Stan Musial one afternoon. "It isn't your position. You've never played there but I'm certain that you can fill the position. Give it a try, Stan."

"Sure," he agreed. "I'll try anything, just as long as I play baseball."

Dyer watched him closely as the converted outfielder took up his infield position. So did Red Schoendienst and Freddie Martin, the keystone combination. But if they had had any worries about how Musial was going to play that all-important position of first base they forgot them quickly.

Stan took to his new post as if he had been born to it. The change in his position did not affect his batting. Stan continued to hammer the ball in his usual great style, and it was he who brought the Cards right back into the hot pennant battle and kept St. Louis in contention for the coveted championship.

On that July 11th against the New York Giants Stan pounded out three hits in four trips to the plate to lead his club to a smashing victory, 13–3.

On July 12 he doubled and scored a run to beat the Giants in the first game of a double-header, 2–1. In the second game Musial whacked out two hits in four times at bat, scoring the winning run in a 5–4 victory over the Giants.

On July 13th Stan continued his slugging, collecting

two more hits and hammering in three runs, but St. Louis couldn't take this one. They lost it, 7–6.

Although Stan Musial's bat had sparked the Cards to three wins over the big New York Giants, unfortunately they had gained no ground on the league-leading Dodgers. Brooklyn had banged out three out of four victories on its own and St. Louis came into Ebbets Field still four and one-half games off the pace.

It was July 14th, and one of the star St. Louis' belter's really great days. A double-header was scheduled and the Brooklyn ball park was jammed to the rafters with rabid Dodger fans yelling for the Cardinal scalp. A double win would put Brooklyn six and one-half games in the lead and could very well give the Dodgers a commanding lead in the pennant fight. Stan Musial and the rest of the Cardinal club had different plans.

In the very first inning of the first game of the double-header Stan walked, reached third base on a hit and an error, then slid under the desperate tag of Bruce Edwards, Dodger catcher, in a brilliant steal of home as St. Louis went in front, 2–0.

The Dodger fans were silent, seeing their dreams vanish—but not for long. Soon the stands were shouting and hollering as Brooklyn tied up the game with a bit of their own fancy slugging. The game was still tied as the Cards came to bat in the eighth inning.

The first two Redbirds were routine outs. Then up stepped Stan Musial to the plate. Always in the midst of every Cardinal threat and rally, Musial sparked the club. This time he hammered out a single and, as usual, his teammates responded. This time it was Enos Slaughter.

"Give that ball a ride!" yelled Eddie Dyer, coaching on the third base side.

Enos Slaughter gave it a ride, all right. He drove the ball clear into Bedford Avenue for a two-run homer, and St. Louis walked off the field with a 5–3 victory. The Dodgers' lead had been cut to three and one-half games.

The second game of that double-header was even more memorable, packed with feverish excitement and great baseball. The Dodgers scored a lone tally early in the game, and with the Brooklyn hurler pitching brilliant shutout ball, that one run loomed up larger and larger as the potential winning margin for the Flock.

There wasn't so much yelling in this game. For seven full innings there was just the tension of that tightly fought pitchers' duel. In the eighth inning, however, the Dodger fans set up a groan as Stan Musial, first man up, larruped the ball against the fences and slid into third base for a stunning triple. Stan came home on Whitey Kurowski's long fly to Dixie Walker, to tie up the game at 1–1.

That was the way the game stood at the end of the regulation nine innings. That's the way the game stood at the end of the tenth inning, the eleventh inning.

Little Vic Lombardi, ace Dodger relief hurler, was pitching for Brooklyn when Stan Musial came up to the plate. Stan wasn't one to waste his swings on bad pitches. He could even wait out a fairly good toss, hoping for the kind of ball he liked. But this time Stan didn't wait. Vic Lombardi took his full windup. Musial swung driving the ball clear out of the park for a tremendous home run, putting the Cards in front 2–1.

That was the way the game ended—2–1. Stan Musial had hammered out two for three in the first game, two more in the second, had been the spark in the first victory and had won the second game. The St. Louis Cardinals were only two and one-half games out of first place.

The next day it was Stan Musial and the Cards again. Manager Leo Durocher started Hugh Casey in the box but Casey didn't last through the first inning. After that it was a parade of pitchers, as Leo used twenty-one men in a vain effort to stop the Cardinals. And it was Musial who was the main culprit, at least as the Dodger fans saw it. He tripled against Ed Head in the fourth inning. He drove Hal Gregg's first pitch in the eighth inning for a two-run homer, his second home run in two days. He hammered out four hits in five times at bat to lead the St. Louis club to a 10–4 victory and put them one and one-half games from the top rung in the league.

Every time he came to the plate the Brooklyn fans set up a moan.

"Stan, the Man," they called him, and no wonder! He was just tearing the vaunted Dodger pitching staff apart. He was the big threat, the difference between victory and defeat, the difference between the pennant and second place.

"Stan, the Man," they christened him in Brooklyn's Ebbets Field, and the name stuck. From then on he was always called Stan, the Man, in every ball park in which he played.

Stan proved his right to that title just a couple of days later. On July 18th the Philadelphia Phillies and the St. Louis Cardinals were battling each other. Ken Raffensberger had come in to hold back the Redbird tide. The score was 4–4 when Stan, the Man, stepped up to bat in the fifth inning and clouted a single into left field.

He edged off first base, stretched his lead, then off like a streak he slid into second base for a clean steal of the bag. He got up, brushed himself off and slid into third base as Enos Slaughter was out on an infield grounder.

Harry Walker was up. He slashed the ball to the infield and Stan was off with the crack of the bat on a daring attempt for the plate and a score. There might have been a play at first, but the Phillies meant to cut down Stan and they played it that way. Stan should have been an easy out.

But they didn't call him the Donora Greyhound for nothing. In a flash, Stan was at home and sliding around the desperate tag of Philadelphia's catcher Andy Seminick.

"Safe!" bawled the umpire at the plate, spreading his hands, and Musial was home with what proved to be the winning run, and the Cardinals moved into first place— ahead of the scrambling, fighting Brooklyn Dodgers.

That lead, however, kept seesawing through the rest of July and August and most of September. When the Chicago Cubs, despite a Musial homer, whipped the Cards 7–2 on September 27th, the Dodgers, who had been idle, climbed back into a flat-footed tie for the lead in the National League. It was the closest race the older baseball circuit had ever witnessed. It was going to be the closest fight in National League history.

The last day of the scheduled race found both clubs still tied. The day before, Joe Hatten had pitched his Dodgers to a 7–4 win over the Braves, as Brecheen, with Stan clouting out another two for four, trimmed the Cubs 4–1.

In the final games of the schedule the Dodgers, tense with the excitement of the race and the importance of victory, played like bush-leaguers and lost. But the Cardinals were just as tense and unsure in the field on that last day, and despite two hits by Stan, one of them a home run, dropped their game to the Cubs by the lop-sided score of 8–3.

The full schedule had been played out and for the first time in the history of organized baseball, the pennant race had ended with two clubs in first place with exactly the same won-and-lost averages. For the first time in baseball history a play-off was necessary to decide the winner of the coveted flag.

Tension in the baseball world was at a peak. Headline newspaper banners called on victory for each city. People gathered at the parks for seats to this classic play-off forty-eight hours before the parks were opened. In Brooklyn there were even prayer meetings and the Dodgers got a special blessing. There was never anything like it in baseball before. There probably never will be again.

17

The first game of that historic play-off was held in St. Louis. Sportsman's Park was jammed with eager fans. They were a noisy, partisan crowd and the yelling started to swell long before the game actually got under way. This was World Series atmosphere—sharp, tense, expectant. In a way it was even greater because this play-off was new to baseball. The excitement mounted until it became almost unbearable.

"Let's go!"

"Belt them out of here!"

"Murder them!"

There was a momentary hush for the singing of "The Star-Spangled Banner" before the game got under way, then a mighty shout which did not let up until the last man was out in the ninth inning.

Ralph Branca, just a year out of New York University and pitching ace for the Brooklyn Dodgers, was on the mound against St. Louis. The Dodger infielders were Stevens at first base, Eddie Stanky at second, Peewee Reese at shortstop, Augie Galan at third, with Bruce Edwards doing the catching. In the outfield for the Dodgers were Dick Whitman, Dixie Walker and Carl Furillo. The Dodgers were the big favorites to win and they were a confident club as they took the field.

For the Cardinals Howie Pollet was on the mound. Joe Garagiola was behind the plate. Musial was at first base, Red Schoendienst was at second base, Marty Marion at short and Whitey Kurowski at third. Patrolling the outfield for the Cardinals were Terry Moore, Dusak and Slaughter.

Pitcher Ralph Branca was good for only two innings. In the third, the Cardinals got to him for two runs and drove him out of the game. Little Vic Lombardi came in to stop the rampant Cards, and he might have done it, too, if it hadn't been for the savage slugging of an inspired Stan Musial.

The Dodgers had come up with a lone tally and the game was still a tossup, the Redbirds leading by the slim margin of 2–1. Then Stan came up to the plate, drove a tremendous triple to the fences and scored on a single by Joe Garagiola. The score was 4–1 in favor of the Cardinals.

The Brooklyn squad didn't give up, however. They managed to push one more run over the plate, but that was all. St. Louis went wild as the Cards dashed off the field with a 4–2 win and the first important victory in the two-out-of-three play-off for the National League pennant.

Brooklyn's Ebbets Field was the scene of the second of those all-important games, and Dodger fans paraded all over the borough with dire threats of what their "Bums" were going to do to the Redbirds.

"Bring them on! You can carry them home!"

"Welcome, St. Louis! Good-by to your pennant!"

If Sportsman's Park in the Mound City had been a scene of wild enthusiasm, it was the calmest spot in the world compared to the mad hooting and hollering that went on in Ebbets Field before the game got started. Once the play got under way, however, a strange silence fell on Brooklyn as the fans watched the progress of the all-important baseball battle.

It was a brilliant pitching duel until the fifth inning. Murray Dickson was pitching two-hit ball for the St. Louis club. Joe Hatten was doing almost as well for the Dodgers. Again the score was 2–1 in favor of the Cards but, as they say in Ebbets Field, anything can happen in Brooklyn.

Joe Hatten disposed of the first two St. Louis batters in the fatal fifth. But then Stan, the Man, stepped up to the plate and the Brooklyn fans groaned. With the count down to three balls and two strikes, Musial drove a screaming liner against the wall for a two-base hit.

Musial's drive over Dixie Walker's head for two bases upset Hatten, the Brooklyn hurler, and he walked Whitey Kurowski. Enos Slaughter, always there to carry on what Stan started, tripled, scoring Stan and Whitey. Dusak singled, scoring Slaughter. The score was 5–1, in favor of St. Louis, and the game was broken wide open.

The Cardinals scored three times again before the game was over, making it 8–1, a runaway. The Dodgers still had some life in them. They finally got to Dickson, who had allowed them a skimpy two hits in eight innings, and belted him for three runs in the ninth. It wasn't enough. The St. Louis Redbirds danced off the field with an 8–4 win and even the Brooklyn fans stayed on to applaud the victorious Cardinals, winners of the first play-off in the history of baseball—1946 champions of the National League.

It was a glorious victory and the Cardinals deserved a well-earned winter's rest. That rest, however, was going to have to wait. There was still a World Series to play and the Cardinals, weary and exhausted by the long fight to win the National League pennant, still had to battle the brilliant Boston Red Sox.

Boston had easily won its championship in the American League. They had had plenty of time to scout the Cardinals. What they saw, of course, didn't frighten them, but they saw enough, especially of Stan Musial, to know that they were in for a rough time.

On the 19th of September a good-sized group of Red Sox players settled themselves comfortably in the Boston Braves ball park to scout the Cardinals who were playing the Boston Braves. Joe Cronin, manager of the American League championship club was there. So was the biggest gun in baseball—Ted Williams.

"He's the greatest hitter in baseball," Stan said admiringly.

There were some who might dispute that statement, giving those laurels to Stan Musial. Certainly they were the number one and number two sluggers in the game, and each had the fullest respect for the other's ability.

Maybe it was because he knew Williams was in the stand that day that the St. Louis slugger put on an exhibition of hitting that Ted Williams and Joe Cronin would never forget.

Musial went to bat five times that afternoon and all he did was drive out five hits. Four times he walloped starting pitcher Mort Cooper, who was now pitching for Boston, for four safeties. His fifth and last hit was against Ray Barrett.

"That's the greatest display of batting I've ever seen," said Ted Williams, full of admiration.

"Hope we don't have to pitch against him," said Cronin.

But it was the Boston Red Sox against the St. Louis Cardinals in the World Series, and a terrific series was expected.

Boston had one of the truly great ball clubs in baseball that year—Ted Williams, Johnny Pesky, Bobby Doerr, Dom DiMaggio and Rudy York. It was a well-balanced, hard-hitting aggregation, and their big bats had hammered the opposing teams in the American League. The Red Sox were further strengthened by a brilliant pitching staff—Ellis Kinder, Mel Parnell, Mickey Harris, Tex Hughson, Boo Ferriss and Joe Dobson. It was a roster strong enough to send fear into the bravest hearts. It served only to heighten the challenge to the St. Louis Cardinals.

"We licked the Dodgers," said Eddie Dyer, flushed with the pennant victory in his first year as a major league manager. "We can lick these American-Leaguers!"

"We'll take four straight," said Enos Slaughter.

"Make it four out of seven," came back Dyer. "I'll take four out of seven. You just go out there and bring back the championship to St. Louis!"

"That we'll do," said Stan Musial.

"That's what I expect," said Eddie. "Now let's go!"

Tex Hughson was on the mound for Boston in the opener of the classic. Howie Pollet opposed him for St. Louis.

More than thirty-six thousand fans jammed Sportsman's Park and saw the Red Sox take the lead in the second inning on a hit batter, a walk and a single. That run looked big as Hughson blanked the Cards in the first five innings.

In the sixth, Schoendienst beat out a hit to first, went to second on Terry Moore's infield out, then Stan, the Man, was up, and hammered the ball against the right field wall for a double, Schoendienst scored and the game was tied. St. Louis scored again in the eighth, when Dom DiMaggio lost the ball in the sun and Whitey Kurowski scored all the way from first. But the game wasn't over.

The Red Sox got that run back in the ninth and Rudy York homered in the tenth to give Boston the first victory in the classic, and the know-it-all tongues began to wag.

"Those Cards are tired after that play-off with Brooklyn."

"Boston is just warming up. They'll take this one in four straight."

The Cards straightened out this talk in a hurry, Harry Brecheen shutting out the Red Sox in the second game with just four hits. St. Louis didn't do much better, collecting only six hits, but those six hits were good for three runs and the ball game. The series was knotted at one victory each. The scene moved to Boston.

In Boston the Red Sox turned the tables on the Cards. This time it was Boo Ferriss who administered the defeat. He pitched great ball, limiting Stan Musial to a single hit in three times at bat, and Boston led again in the series, two victories to one.

With Tex Hughson in the pitchers' box, looking for his second victory, it did begin to look like a hopeless cause. But the Cards pulled a surprise again, this time with a vengeance. They slugged Bosox pitching for an amazing total of twenty hits and ran off with the game by the lopsided score of 12–3. St. Louis was in the series and they meant to win it.

But World Series competition, a short series, is mighty unpredictable. One day one team is up there, sure to win. The next day it's the other club. The 1946 classic ran true to form, as Joe Dobson pitched a masterful game, cutting down the Redbird bats to size and limiting the club to four hits, one of them by Musial, and won easily, 6–3.

Again, as in 1926 and 1934 in their past history, the Cards were just one game away from losing the World Series. But the resiliency of the Redbirds was demonstrated again as they battered the Bosox to a 4–1 win and brought the decision in the classic down to the last game of the series.

Murray Dickson pitched for St. Louis, Ferriss for the Bosox, as the game started. Boston immediately jumped to a one-run lead in the first inning. St. Louis came back with a single tally in the second. In the fifth inning the Cards belted Ferriss out of the game, scoring two runs and taking a 3–1 lead. But in the eighth inning the Bosox got to Dickson, hammering him off the mound, and Dom DiMaggio doubled off Harry Brecheen—sending in two runs to tie the score again.

The Cards, however, were not to be denied. They came back in the same eighth, with some great running by Enos Slaughter and scored on an eyelash play at the plate. It was the run which spelled the difference between the champion and the also-ran. It was the run which won the game and the World Series. The Bosox got two men on base in the ninth. An attempted bunt resulted in a force-out at second. Partee fouled to Stan Musial who made a great running catch and whipped the ball into the plate to keep Rudy York from trying to score from third. Then McBride sent a roller to Red Schoendienst. The ball rolled up his arm and the fans let out a mighty moan. But Red recovered the ball, snapped it to Stan Musial and McBride was out and the Cardinals were World Champions.

It was a great year for freshman manager Eddie Dyer.

It was a great year for the St. Louis Cardinals. It was one of the greatest years in the baseball career of the Donora Greyhound, Stan, the Man—Musial.

For the second time in four years of big-league ball, Stan hammered out over two hundred hits—two hundred twenty-eight, to be exact. He led the league in this department. He also led the league in doubles, for the third time, with fifty. He was the league leader in triples with twenty. He led the league in most runs scored with one hundred twenty-four. For the second time in his major league career he was the champion batter of the National League with a great .365 batting average.

It was a foregone conclusion that the man who had batted and sparked his club to the National League pennant and the World Championship, would be voted the Most Valuable Player in the National League. He was. Of the twenty-four sports writers voting for the Most Valuable Player award, twenty-two named Stan Musial to first place. One writer placed him second to his teammate Enos Slaughter. In all, Musial was voted three hundred nineteen of a possible three hundred thirty-six points, one hundred seventy-seven points ahead of his nearest rival, Dixie Walker of the Brooklyn Dodgers. No man was ever more deserving of the honor. He was the first man, incidentally, in the National League to have received the award at two different positions. He had played the outfield for his 1943 plaque. He was a converted first baseman when he won the plaque in 1946. Only one other man in big-league ball had done that before—Hank Greenberg of the American League, first at first base, then, to reverse Stan's record, in the outfield.

Nor was that the end of the awards for his feats of 1946. On January 25th, during the ensuing winter, the

New York Chapter of the Baseball Writers' Association
of America met to bestow still another prize on the young
athlete. They awarded him one of the most treasured
trophies of the game, the Sid Mercer Memorial Award,
and named him Player of the Year.

The Philadelphia Sports Writers Association went the
New Yorkers one better. At a special dinner for one
thousand one hundred players and writers and sports
magnates, the sports writers of the Friendly City went all
out and named Stan Musial the Outstanding Athlete of
the Year 1946. It was a tremendous year for the young
star. In five short years he leaped to the very top of the
baseball world.

Stan had had a terrific season. There were more great
seasons ahead. The year 1947, however, was to bring a
change of pace. It was to bring about a turn of events
that threatened to cut short the brilliant career of Stan
Musial.

CHAPTER 18

The big welcome mat was spread out for Stan Musial, when he arrived, late, at the spring training camp of the St. Louis Cardinals in St. Petersburg, Florida.

"Good to see you, Stan!" hollered Eddie Dyer.

For a while back, there had been some question as to whether Stan was going to show up or not. There had been some difference between owner Sam Breadon and the Most Valuable Player in the National League as to what the St. Louis club ought to be paying for its star slugger.

"Pasquel offered me thirty thousand dollars a year to play for the Mexican League," said Stan. "He threw in a seventy-five thousand dollar bonus."

"Look what's happened to the Mexican League," countered Breadon, and he had a point. The Mexican League had folded quickly and the men who had jumped out of their National and American League contracts were clamoring to get back into the good graces of American baseball.

"All right," agreed Musial. "I'm not asking for any seventy-five thousand dollars, but I'm worth a lot more than that fifteen thousand dollars you paid me last year."

"How much?" asked Breadon.

That's where the argument threatened to bog down. Sam Breadon, generous enough in his own right, had some sort of mental block about paying any kind of real money to his ballplayers. And Stan Musial was just as adament about getting a contract which really measured up to his value as a ballplayer.

For a while it looked as though the owner of the ball club and his ace player would never get together. Sports headlines screamed:

STAN MUSIAL HOLDOUT

MUSIAL SENDS BACK CONTRACT

MUSIAL AND BREADON IN CONTRACT HASSLE

"St. Louis in spring training in Florida, but Stan Musial isn't around," read one sports story.

"Why doesn't Sam Breadon loosen his purse strings and pay Stan Musial the kind of money that's coming to him?" asked a sports columnist.

The pressure was on Breadon, but Sam was a tough businessman. For a long, long time, he sat tight in St. Louis and Stan just lingered on in Donora, while Manager Eddie Dyer sweated it out in St. Petersburg.

Then, abruptly, there was a long conference in the St. Louis front offices, with Sam Breadon at one end of the table, Stan at the other; and like all arguments about baseball contracts, the long debate between the two men came to an end on a compromise. Stan Musial was back in the Cardinal's fold. Eddie Dyer shook the star slugger's hand.

"Sure glad you're back with us!" said Eddie, slapping Stan's broad back.

Stan grinned.

"Glad to be back myself," he said.

"We need you here!" yelled the ebullient Eddie. "We need that big stick of yours! A good many of the ball clubs are stronger this year.

And then, for the first time, Eddie noticed that there was something different about Musial. He couldn't quite put his finger on it, but he didn't react properly on the field. He was pale and listless.

"You've lost weight, Stan," he said abruptly.

"Just a little."

"You've been working in the mills?" asked the manager.

"Why?" came back Stan, a bit irritated with the cross-examination. "A man can work anywhere he pleases. Why did you say that?"

"Forget it," said Eddie quickly. "You look kind of tired."

"I just got off the train," snapped the usually affable Musial.

"Sure," said Dyer, trying to calm him down, and Stan grinned, embarrassed.

"Just give me a couple of days," he said. "I'll be sunburned like the rest of you."

"Yeah," agreed Eddie, but he wasn't sure. "We'll get that weight back on you, too," he added, but he was puzzled.

The manager had more reason to be worried as spring training moved along. There was something different about Stan Musial in 1947. He had always been a slow starter in spring training, but this year he just didn't seem to be able to get started at all.

"You all right, Stan?" he asked the slugger a dozen times.

"I'm all right," Stan snapped back, but the Donora Greyhound wasn't all right, and no one knew it better than he.

Things got worse when the pennant race got under

way. St. Louis, 1946 World Champions, began its 1947 season by splitting its first four games, and Stan did nothing to help win those two games, either. This was no way for champions to start a pennant battle, no way for a batting champion to start his season. But this was only the beginning. The Cardinals, with Stan Musial looking pale and sickly, playing listlessly, lost nine straight games. By the first week in May, they were deep in the cellar and Musial was hitting a woeful .174.

"What's the matter with Musial?" wrote the sports writers.

"Come on, Stan!" pleaded the St. Louis fans.

Eddie Dyer angrily tossed his cap on the floor in the Cardinal clubhouse.

"You're playing like a bunch of bush-leaguers! Champs! You couldn't beat a sandlot team the way you've been swinging your bats! Bushers!"

Stan Musial sat quietly on his bench. There was nothing he could say. A dull but constant pain in his stomach told him that something was seriously wrong with him, but he said nothing.

And St. Louis kept losing ball games.

By the middle of May Stan's batting average had plummeted down to .164. By May 19th he had dropped to .140. The baseball world just couldn't believe it.

"He just hasn't got it any more. He's all washed up," a fan stormed.

"Can't be."

"It's happened before. A player goes great one year, the next year he's all through. Just a flash in the pan."

"Not Stan Musial. It just can't happen to Stan."

But it did. Twenty-two times straight Stan went up to bat and failed to hit safely. Then one day the fans were treated to a rarity—the slugger Musial was trying to bunt to break his batting slump.

"Maybe you're right," the Cardinal fans began to admit. "Maybe he's through."

"He's through all right, but I hate to see him go."

Eddie Dyer was bewildered. The fans were stunned by this unexpected and sudden reversal in the fortunes of their great hero. Stan suffered in silence, and the pain in his stomach wouldn't let up. He couldn't relax, eat or sleep.

Finally it happened. Stan sat on the edge of his bed in his hotel room brooding on his loss of power, fighting against the ache in his stomach. Then, suddenly, he crumpled and collapsed in a heap at the foot of his bed.

There was no one in the room to call for help.

"I don't know how long I was unconscious," he said later. "All I know is that when I did come to I was just doubled up with pain."

"Why didn't you tell me about this before?" yelled Eddie Dyer. "Why didn't you open up? You get back to St. Louis!" he ordered. "Dr. Hyland will fix you up in no time."

For the first time in the 1947 season Eddie Dyer saw some daylight ahead.

Dr. Robert Francis Hyland, the St. Louis surgeon, was not too sure. "You've got an inflamed appendix," he said to Stan. "You've had it for a long time. I don't see how you could have played any kind of ball. You're lucky it didn't rupture. Why in heaven's name did you play with this pain? Didn't you know it was dangerous?"

"I wanted to play as long as I could," said Stan. "What do I do now?"

"I'll have to operate," the doctor told him.

"How long will I be out of the game?"

"A couple of months anyway," replied Dr. Hyland.

Stan thought for a minute. "Isn't there some other way?" he asked.

"We could feed you penicillin," the doctor said.

"How do you mean that?" asked Stan eagerly.

"If we give you enough penicillin shots, and regularly enough, you might go on playing."

"How do you mean 'might go on playing'?"

"Sometimes an appendix will burst. That means trouble."

"And sometimes it doesn't," countered Musial.

"That's right," said Dr. Hyland.

"I'll take the penicillin!" declared Stan. "The ball club needs me. I can't stay out of the line-up too long. The players are counting on me. I can't let them down."

"You're taking quite a risk," warned the doctor. "That appendix can burst and kill you."

"I can't let the club down," Stan repeated. "I'll take that risk!"

Dr. Hyland fed Stan penicilin and it worked wonders for the determined young ballplayer.

By the middle of June Stan had pushed his batting average up to .202. The Cardinals were still in last place. By the end of June he was hitting .253.

He received a telegram from Dick Kerr. "You're a natural .300 hitter," he read. "Keep slugging the ball. I'm with you all the way." The man who had been more responsible than anyone else for keeping Stan in baseball had not forgotten him. The telegram gave Stan a tremendous boost.

By the end of July Stan had climbed to a .282 average and St. Louis was in second place.

"The way Stan goes," said the fans, "that's the way St. Louis goes."

The sports writers went the fans one better. "Stan Musial is a one-man ball club."

By the middle of August Musial was hitting in the charmed .300 circle and the Cardinals were fighting the Brooklyn Dodgers once more for the National League pennant. However, they never caught up with them. That long slump in April and May was too big a hurdle to overcome. It was a minor baseball miracle that they could come up as far as they did, and that baseball miracle was due to Stan Musial.

After the poorest possible start, the Donora Greyhound had pounded his way back into the leading hitters' list. After sinking as low as .140, he wound up the season with a prodigious streak of spectacular hitting. He batted for an average of well over .400 in the last months of the season and wound up with a total of one hundred and eighty-three hits, thirty of them doubles, thirteen triples and nineteen home runs, more home runs than he had ever hit before in the National League. He batted in ninety-five runs, scored one hundred and thirteen. His average for the season was .312,

It was a great comeback for the St. Louis star. A .312 batting average was considerably below the kind of batting Stan had been giving baseball, but it's an average that is more than good enough to keep a ballplayer in the big leagues. There was, however, a curious reaction to Stan's .312 batting.

"That was a pretty sad year you had," said a reporter to Stan, reminiscing at one of the baseball winter dinners.

"Sure was," agreed Stan, recalling those agonizing spring months.

A few minutes later the reporter was reminded that Stan had hit for a mighty .312 average, and he was quick to apologize.

"Say, you hit pretty well there in 1947," said the red-faced scribe. "You did a lot better than .300."

"I guess I did," agreed Stan modestly.

"I wouldn't call .312 a sad batting average," continued the writer. "How many ballplayers hit three hundred last year?"

"Not many, I guess," put in Stan.

"You can bet your boots there weren't many," said the reporter, trying to make up for his boner. Then he smiled broadly with sudden understanding, and his embarrassment was all gone. "I get it," he continued. "A .312 average may be all right for pretty nearly any other ballplayer. It's not good enough for Stan Musial."

During the winter Dr. Hyland operated on Stan and removed the appendix. Stan rested up. He did nothing but loaf and enjoyed every minute romping with his children. His son Richard was growing fast. He was six years old and Geraldine, his daughter, was three. The children loved to walk through the streets of Donora with their popular father, and Stan spent every waking hour with his family.

Then abruptly the winter passed, the snow melted away. Spring was in the air. Stan packed his bags, said good-by to his family and reported to the Cardinals' training camp in Florida.

19

Stan began to belt the ball right at the start of the 1948 season. He was eager to make up for that "poor" 1947 year and he went at the opposing hurlers with all the power and skill he possessed. This was the year he meant to regain the batting crown and he got off to a tremendous start.

On April 30th he gave an exhibition of batting the Cincinnati fans would long remember. At bat five times, Stan blasted the Redleg hurlers for five base hits. Two of them were singles, two doubles, one a home run. He had begun to put more power into his drives.

For some time now, they had been comparing the slugger with the all-time great hitters in baseball. They were comparing him especially with the powerhouse on the Boston Red Sox club, Ted Williams.

"Ted hits the long ball," one writer said.

"That's right, but Stan can place them anywhere."

"Williams gets more extra bases."

"Stan gets on base as often as Williams any time. And didn't he win the league slugging championship in 1943, 1944, 1945 and 1946?"

Back and forth they argued the respective merits of the players.

"Give me that homer Williams comes up with in the pinch."

"I'll take Stan Musial and his doubles and triples—and yes, those singles, too!"

On one thing all fans and ballplayers and writers were

agreed. Ted Williams was top man in the American League, Stan Musial in the National League. As for Stan, he just let the argument rage. It made little difference to him who was considered the greater batter. His interest was in playing the game to the best of his ability. He was not playing for his own glory. He didn't play for the grandstand, he was a team man. He was actually beginning to hit the longer ball more often. He was getting those home runs more often. As a matter of fact, right through that 1948 season he was either leading or just right back of the leader in the home run slugging department.

"Belt it, Stan!"

And he did.

"Smack it out of the park, Musial!"

He did that, too.

On May 19th St. Louis played the Dodgers and Stan was in top form. He always batted well against the tough Brooklyn club. On this day he hammered them unmercifully. Stan went to bat six times that afternoon. He belted Brooklyn pitching for three singles, a double and a triple. They walked him the sixth time he swung his bat menacingly in the direction of Bedford Avenue. This was Stan's second five for five at the bat in the young season.

The next day, May 20th, the Dodger fans were cheering Stan every time he got up to the plate. It is a strange phenomenon, but true, that Stan gets more applause from the fans in Brooklyn's Ebbets Field than anywhere else. This, despite the fact that Musial has cost the Dodgers the pennant in at least four battles for the flag.

"Here's that man!" yelled the admiring Brooklyn fans, and Stan answered their greetings with another big hit.

On May 19th Stan got three singles, a double and a

triple in Ebbets Field. The next day he cracked out a single, a couple of doubles and a big home run.

On June 22nd Musial splattered the fences for five straight singles against the high-riding Boston Braves.

"That makes it four," wrote the sport scribes. "The man who holds the record for the most five-for-fives in the big leagues is the Number One man in the Hall of Fame—Ty Cobb." Cobb got five hits in five at bats on exactly five occasions. It was one of those fantastic records that are seldom topped. Musial had gotten four such days, and the fans and experts were rooting for him to equal Cobb's great record.

"Musial is a great batter, maybe the greatest of them all," wrote another scribe. "He's sure to match Ty Cobb's record sooner or later, but the odds are against his doing it this season. Stan has already collected four five-for-fives this year. It isn't likely he'll get another."

Even the sports writers had to hedge on their predictions. Stan Musial was traveling at such a terrific clip that nothing was impossible at the moment.

Stan read the sports pages, of course, but the speculation concerning Cobb's record didn't trouble him. He was having another great year and the team was playing good ball.

St. Louis was playing in Boston toward the tail end of the season and it was one of those late September days, September 22nd to be exact, when the wind kicks up and there is a chill in the air. It wasn't especially good weather for baseball, but it didn't bother Stan. There was something else troubling him, however.

"Looks like your wrists are swollen, Stan," said manager Eddie Dyer, looking his big fellow over.

"It's nothing," said Stan.

"It doesn't look like nothing to me," snapped Eddie. "Better get back into the clubhouse and let Doc take a look at them."

"I'll see him after the game," said Stan, beginning to trot out onto the field.

"You'll see him now!" yelled Eddie Dyer, stopping him.

Stan pulled up short, flexed his fingers.

"I want to get into the game," he said. "I want to play ball. I'll see Doc later."

Eddie studied his man, finally broke into a grin.

"You'd want to play with both wrists broken."

Stan laughed but there was nothing to laugh about.

Actually his wrists pained him sharply. He couldn't flex his fingers without getting that quick, sharp ache.

"All right," agreed Stan. "I'll have Doc strap them up for me."

"Maybe you ought to take the day off," suggested Dyer, giving the wrists another look.

"Maybe I ought to take the rest of the season off," offered Stan, as he ran back into the clubhouse.

Doc Weaver strapped the swollen wrists but the pain was still there.

He didn't tell that to Doc. He didn't tell that to Eddie Dyer, either.

"Fine!" he said, holding up his two hands for inspection, then walked over for his bat and his first trip to the plate.

Boston was going great guns at the moment. They had won eight straight. They were heading for the pennant. Warren Spahn, ace Brave hurler, was out there to make it nine straight.

Stan watched a couple of balls come in over the plate. His wrists ached; the tape around them wasn't going to help the snap of his swing; he knew he wasn't going to be able to pull the ball. The count was two and two and Musial hadn't offered at a pitch. Spahn took his windup, tossed in a fast one and Stan drove it into left field for a clean single.

When he came up for his second at bat, he had ripped the tape off his wrists. The wrists hurt but he couldn't bat the way he wanted to with the bandages on them.

Spahn was still in the box and Stan waited him out again. He wasn't offering at any kind of pitch. Every time he swung his bat the pain in his wrists would shoot right through him.

Again the count went up, this time to three balls and two strikes, and again Stan swung. This time he drove the ball over the head of the left fielder and raced to second base with a double.

Warren Spahn was out of the game and Ray Barrett was doing the pitching when Musial stepped up to bat in the fourth inning. Barrett whipped a fast ball across the plate and Musial, with a mighty swing, drove the ball into the right field bull pen for his thirty-eighth home run of the season and his third straight hit in the ball game.

Clyde Shoun was the next Braves' pitcher in the big parade that afternoon as Stan came up for his fourth time at bat. He dragged himself to the batter's box and took his stance facing the pitcher. The pain was so intense he couldn't stand up straight. He faced Shoun in a crouch, bent over the plate.

He watched a couple of fast balls come in. He just couldn't afford to take a waste swing. Then he whacked an inside pitch just between second and short. Alvin Dark made a diving stab at the ball, but it was through, and

Stan Musial was on first base with his fourth straight hit of the day.

"Four for four, Stan," said Red Schoendiensst, as they sat on the bench.

"Yeah," said Stan, not thinking, nursing the terrible ache in his wrists.

"Next time you get up to bat—and hit," said Enos Slaughter, "you tie Ty Cobb's record."

"How's that?"

Stan was suddenly alert. For a moment he forgot his aches and pains.

"Sure," pitched in Marty Marion. "You've got four five-for-fives. One more hit and you make Cobb's record."

"Yeah," said Stan. "Sure. Gosh, I didn't realize it."

But he was thinking of the pain in his wrists again, wondering how he could possibly get another hit.

"You can do it, Stan!" yelled Whitey Kurowski.

"You've got to!" said Eddie Dyer.

"Sure thing, Skipper," said Musial, but he didn't know how.

Al Lyons was in the box when Stan came up for that fateful fifth trip to the plate. Lyons was a right-handed pitcher but he was as wild as the wildest southpaw.

Stan watched the first ball come in—sharp and wide of the plate. Stabs of pain danced through his aching wrists and body.

"Ball one!" howled the umpire.

"Get is over the plate!" scowled Red Schoendienst.

The second pitch was wide.

"Ball two!"

Stan got the idea that Lyons was going to purposely walk him. So did the rest of the Cardinal bench.

"Pitch that ball!" yelled Slaughter.

"Get it over!" snapped Marion.

The whole Cardinal club was standing on the edge of the dugout.

"Get it in there!" yelled Ron Northey.

Al Lyons was minding his own business. He took his full windup, then let go with a fast one.

It takes less than a second, or so it seems, before the pitch reaches the plate, and the batter has less time than that to decide on whether to take or hit. Stan had decided in less time than that. He was going to swing at anything that his bat could reach.

Lyons had thrown him a bad pitch. It was off and wide but Stan, aching wrists and all, swung at the ball, hammered it between first and second, then streaked into first base, safe, with five hits for five times at bat. Fans and players alike let out a mighty yell, a great ovation for a great player.

Stan had belted out his fourth five-for-five of the season, his fifth five-for-five in his career. He had matched the great Ty Cobb's record! And he had accomplished it despite aching wrists. Somehow the pain lessened and soon he forgot that awful ordeal.

In six hundred and eleven trips to the plate. Stan Musial drove out two hundred and thirty safe blows. He was the leader by far in that department. He had banged out eighteen triples and he led his league in that, too. Only by the narrowest of margins did Stan miss making it a clean sweep. Never before a home run hitter, Stan smashed thirty-nine homers in 1948, just one home run behind Johnny Mize and Ralph Kiner, who were tied with forty each for the home run crown of the year. It was an astounding exhibition of batting the Donora Greyhound had put on for the fans that year.

Stan batted in one hundred and thirty-one runs that tremendous season, leading the league in that area. He also led the league with one hundred and thirty-five runs scored. He led the league in total bases for the third time in his career. He was the slugging champion for the third time, too, this year with the terrific percentage of .702, the first time since Hack Wilson in 1930 that any batter had bettered the .700 mark.

His batting average for the year was a scintillating .376. St. Louis hadn't won the pennant and Johnny Sain's sensational pitching had brought the flag to Boston for the first time in twenty-four years. Still, when it came to selecting the Most Valuable Player in the National League for 1948, Stan Musial was the sports writers' choice by a big margin—three hundred and three votes to two hundred and twenty-three. It was a well-earned tribute. The great St. Louis slugger had won his third Most Valuable Player Award in the National League Plaque. He was the first ballplayer in the league to be so signally honored. Carl Hubbell and Stan had previously shared the honor of being the only two-time winners of the senior league. Now Stan stood alone, the three-time winner. He was the biggest name in National League ball.

CHAPTER 20

The year 1948 was a brilliant, a happy one, for Stan Musial. It was a year, however, which also brought the first touch of tragedy into his life.

In the winter of 1948 Papa Lukasz passed away. Lukasz Musial had been a good father, a hard worker, a man who wanted everything for his children and gave everything he had to them. The poor immigrant, who came from Poland to the New World to build a better life for his family, had given all his strength and all his energy in that direction.

"I want you to go to college," he had said to Stan. "I want you to be a good, educated American. I want you to become a professional man, to live a better life than I did."

His goodness and his dreams rubbed off on his children. While Stan didn't go to college, he got an education in the rugged school of professional baseball. He had fulfilled his father's dream of a better life for his son, a professional life. Papa Lukasz had fought against Stan's going into baseball, but he had lived long enough to see Stan become one of the most admired and beloved men in American public life.

"I'm glad," said Stan, "that I could help him realize, even a little, something of his dreams."

"You did more than that," said his wife, consoling the grief-stricken Musial. "You made him feel that he had done a good job, that he had paid back part of his debt to America."

"I'm twenty-eight years old," said Stan. "I'd better take stock of my life."

"You're still a very young fellow," said Lil.

"I've got a wife and two children to think of."

They were sitting in the living room, quietly talking over the intimate things which concern any family. The death of Papa Lukasz made the moment, however, more sober than usual.

"I've got to think of my mother, too," said Musial.

"We're doing very well, Stan," offered Lil quietly.

"Sure, I'm doing all right," countered Musial, "but for how long? How long do you think I can play ball?"

"What are you thinking?" asked Lil, suddenly disturbed by Stan's mood.

Stan got up from his chair, walked to the window.

"I'm not going to play baseball forever," he said. "Nobody can play baseball forever."

Lil knew how deeply Stan had been affected by his father's death. She waited for her husband to say whatever was on his mind, for she realized he had to talk, just to loosen all the tensions in him.

Stan walked the floor again, restlessly.

"We've got to begin thinking of the future. We just can't go on living this way, without planning. After all," he hesitated, "I'm not going to be around here always!"

"What are you talking about?" snapped Lil, suddenly coming alive.

"We've all got to die sometime!" Stan shouted. "I can't live forever. I want to be sure that you and the kids have something to live on when I go!"

Lil couldn't answer. She was all choked up and the tears ran down her face.

"Sorry," snapped Stan, seeing what he had done to his wife. He put his arms around her, comfortingly.

"Sorry," he repeated.

"That's all right, Stan," said Lil, finally finding her voice. "You're just upset. Let's talk about this some other time."

But Stan was determined to speak his mind.

"I was just thinking, Lil," he began again, more soberly, "that maybe I ought to look around, find some other way of making a living. Baseball is a funny game. Today I'm a hero. Next year I may be out of it. My batting falls off, or I get hurt. . . ."

"Don't talk about getting hurt!"

"Those things happen."

"You're not going to get hurt!" insisted Lil.

"All right," agreed Stan, grinning for the first time that evening, "so I won't get hurt. I'll play till I'm ninety. But what happens after I'm ninety."

Lil was smiling, too, now.

"You could be a sports announcer on the radio, like Joe DiMaggio, Dizzy Dean, Bob Feller. They do very well on the air."

"Sure, sure," consented Stan, serious again, "but that's not for me."

"Why not?" queried his proud young wife. "I'd like to hear you on the radio. You'd sound good."

"Not me," grinned the embarrassed ballplayer. "I couldn't give out the way Dizzy does, or the way Bob does. Those fellows can talk at the drop of the hat. You know how I am when it comes to talking."

"The silent kind."

"I guess so," admitted Stan, smiling again. "Can't help that, can I?"

Lil thought for a minute.

"Maybe you can be a silent partner? There's always a silent partner in every business somewhere. You could be a silent partner, couldn't you?"

Lil was doing a little teasing on her own, but there was also a good bit of truth in what she was saying.

"I think you've got something," said Stan.

"I know I've got something," said Lil.

"I'll look around," Stan suggested.

"Just let the word get around," said his wife. "You'll get an offer quick, and a good one, too."

Lillian was right. Stan let a couple of sports writers know that he was looking for a business interest outside of baseball. An offer came quickly.

"I've got a deal for you, Stan," said Julius "Biggie" Garagnani, a St. Louis restaurateur and a great admirer of the Cardinal slugger. "I think we would make a fine business team."

"I'm listening to any sound offer," said Stan.

"Let's open a restaurant together," said Biggie.

Stan looked a bit bewildered.

"What do I know about restaurants? I'm a ballplayer. I don't know anything about the food business."

"Sure, you're a ballplayer," agreed Biggie, "the best. And I'm the best restaurant man in St. Louis."

"So what?"

"So you keep belting them out for the Cardinals, and I'll run the restaurant."

"That's fine. So why do you need me?"

"I'll tell you," explained Biggie. "I've got a fine location. I know the exact spot. We put up a big sign: STAN MUSIAL'S AND BIGGIE'S STEAK HOUSE. Everybody comes to see Stan Musial. Everybody comes to eat Biggie's steak. It's a sure thing."

"Sounds good," concurred Stan, "but how can I be in the restaurant when I'm batting the ball in Ebbets Field?"

Biggie Garagnani laughed.

"You just drop in when you're playing in St. Louis. That'll be more than good enough. How about it, Stan? If business is good, you move the family to St. Louis."

"Give me a couple of days."

"Sure. Take your time."

"I want to talk it over with my wife."

"Good thing."

Lil hopped on the idea fast.

"It's what you wanted, isn't it? This is the business to give us that security you wanted. Fine. You call up Biggie and call it a deal."

Stan went into business and the restaurant flourished. He made friends easily, and he and Biggie attracted the most influential people in St. Louis. It became the gathering place for all outstanding dinner events in town. Stan Musial was glad to be part owner of the restaurant —he needed to know that his family was secure, that they would never be financially pressed as he had been when he was a boy growing up in the poverty of the mill town of Donora.

The restaurant gave Stan a lift. It also had a curiously indirect effect on the baseball season of 1949.

CHAPTER 21

"Here comes the big restaurateur!" hollered Red Schoendienst, greeting Musial at the Card training camp in the spring of 1949.

"How are the steaks doing?" asked Freddie Martin.

Stan grinned good-naturedly.

"Feel my muscle!" he ordered. "This is going to bang out a lot of home runs!"

"Never saw a cow hit a home run!" sniped Enos Slaughter.

"You're going to see me hit them!" came back Stan.

There was a lot of banter in the camp, but Musial was more serious about those home runs than his teammates might have thought.

"I hit thirty-nine last year," said the Redbird slugger. "Just one short of Johnny Mize and Ralph Kiner. Don't see why I can't beat them out this year."

"You can do it," said Eddie Dyer thoughtfully, "but you won't be getting as many hits."

"I hit thirty-nine without aiming for the fences," put in Stan.

"Sure," agreed Eddie. "You can get them that way. But once you start driving for the stands, you're going to change your swing. Your timing is going to be different. You'll be pressing all the time, going for that home run."

But Stan, like all young ballplayers, was determined to match and beat all the great records in baseball. He didn't talk about it. It wasn't a personal thing. It wasn't that he wanted the personal glory. It was just the business of playing the game to the best of his ability.

"I'd like to win that home run crown just once," he admitted to his roommate and pal Red Schoendienst. "Red, I just feel that if I try hard enough I can win that title, don't you?"

"Sure," Red agreed. "You can do it, too, I guess."

"I can give it a try anyway," said Stan, taking an imaginary cut at an imaginary ball.

He had conquered all the other heights in baseball batting. And he had conquered that small sense of insecurity which had always been with him by joining Biggie in the restaurant business. For once he really felt utterly free, and from the start of the season Stan went after that long ball. The results were almost disastrous.

Every time Musial came to bat he swung for the fences. He was digging himself deeper into the box. He was trying for greater distance, more pull on every swing. He was disturbing and upsetting that magnificent sense of timing in his swing that had won for him so many batting honors.

"Something wrong with my timing," he said, sitting down in the dugout.

Eddie Dyer had told him that would happen but he said nothing as he sat next to the disturbed ballplayer.

"I don't meet the ball squarely," said Stan. "I don't meet it at all. I haven't gotten any decent hits in a week."

And that was a fact. By the middle of May the slugger who had batted his way to the league championship with a tremendous .376, was now hitting the ball for an anemic average of .253.

"Can't get started," complained Stan.

"Stop trying for the fences," said Dyer at last. "Just get up there and hit the ball. Forget those home runs and you'll be batting what you ought to bat. Just get up there, Stan, and concentrate on meeting the ball."

"Yeah," said Stan. "I guess you're right."

"I know I'm right!" snapped the Cardinal skipper, and he walked off the bench, leaving Stan to stew in his own disappointment.

Musial was down to the park early the next day, taking a long batting practice session in the batting cage.

Eddie Dyer caught his eye but said nothing.

That afternoon Stan forgot about the long ball, concentrated on meeting it, but he didn't have much luck.

He was in the park early the next morning, and the morning after, taking his swings in the practice cage.

"It takes a while to get back into your normal batting stride," said Eddie Dyer.

On July 6, 1949, Jackie Robinson, the great Dodger second baseman, was coming into his own. As the first Negro ballplayer in the big leagues, for two years he had fought a long personal battle with tradition and prejudice. This year he was the full-grown star, leading the league with a great .362 batting average, twenty-four points in front of Red Schoendienst. Stan Musial wasn't even among the first ten batters in the league.

"You're a natural .300 hitter," Dick Kerr had written to the St. Louis player in 1947, and Stan would never forget it. That steady batting practice was going to help. The fact that he could forget his drive for the home run crown would help. What helped most, however, was a particular nasty article by a thoroughly misinformed, if not downright nasty, sports writer.

"The reason Stan Musial isn't hitting this year," wrote the scribe, "is the Stan Musial and Biggie's Steak House in southwest St. Louis. Stan put a lot of money into that restaurant and it isn't very busy. The erstwhile Cardinal slugger stands to lose a big chunk of cash in that eating venture. He's too worried about business when he should be thinking of baseball. That's why last year's leading batter is going exactly nowhere in 1949."

Stan resented the article, but he bore no hard feelings toward the scribe.

"Makes his living writing, doesn't he?" he said. "Maybe he had nothing else to write about."

"But how about it?" pressed another reporter. "How about that restaurant?"

Stan scowled.

"How about it? It's going great! It's packing them in every night. Wish I was doing as well as the Steak House. I'd be batting .400!"

Stan was angry about the sports story. He took his anger out on the ball. That afternoon he belted the opposition for two line-drive singles and a tremendous triple.

"That's hitting them, Stan," yelled Red Schoendienst.

"That's the boy!" hollered Marty Marion.

Eddie Dyer sat quietly in the dugout, controlling the small smile of satisfaction. Stan Musial had begun to hit. He was going to keep hitting—and St. Louis was back in the fight for the pennant again.

By July 6th Stan Musial wasn't to be counted among the ten leading hitters in the National League and the Cardinals were floating around in the mire of seventh place. On July 10th the big Redbird gun began to boom and the St. Louis club began to move up. Stan got one for five in the first game of the double-header against the Cincinnati Redlegs. He got two for five in the second game, scored three times for his club—and St. Louis had whipped the Redlegs twice, 4–2 and 7–4.

Stan's bat really got loose in the 1949 All-Star game, the annual clash between the greatest players in both the American and National Leagues. Musial had been the choice of both the sport scribes and the fans in their yearly poll to select the casts for these stellar battles. He had played in every All-Star game from his very first year in the big time, with the exception of the one year he had been in the United States Navy. In the 1949 All-Star game, Musial was the outstanding individual performer.

The American League line-up read like a future list for the Hall of Fame: Dom DiMaggio, George Kell, Ted Williams, Joe DiMaggio, Eddie Joost, Ed Robinson, Cass Michaels, Birdie Tebbetts, Mel Parnell, Vic Raschi. The National League roster for the game matched the junior league roster for sheer brilliance. There was league-leading hitter Jackie Robinson, the first Negro in the All-Star classic. There was Stan Musial, of course. Home-run kings Ralph Kiner and Johnny Mize. There were George Marshall, Eddie Kazak, Andy Seminick, George Munger, Preacher Roe and Warren Spahn. The pitchers were great. The sluggers were greater. The 1949 All-Star game was a tremendous slugging match.

Spahn fanned both Dom DiMaggio and Ted Williams in the first inning, but George Kell, Joe DiMaggio, Birdie Tebbetts and Ed Robinson cracked through with four runs, and the American League squad was off to a great start.

Jackie Robinson singled and then Stan Musial brought the great crowd to its feet with a prodigous home run clout to bring the National League team back into the ball game.

Robinson walked in the third inning. Stan got his second hit of the afternoon, a scorching single, to send Robinson to third. Kiner hit into a double play but Jackie scored and the game was 4–3 in favor of the American League.

Stan blasted another hit for himself to make it three for four against the toughest American League pitching. And although the National-Leaguers amassed seven runs it wasn't enough. The American League scored eleven and took the game.

St. Louis, like the rest of the National League clubs, was sorely disappointed about that loss, but there was one big saving item in the game. Stan had had his greatest All-Star game. He was certainly out of the long slump which had bogged him down the entire first half of the 1949 season.

By the 22nd of July Stan had pushed his batting average up to .293 and the Cards were battling the Dodgers again for the lead in the pennant race. As a matter of fact, they came into Brooklyn that day for a night game just two and one-half games off the lead. It was a series that veteran sports writers call the greatest individual series that Stan Musial ever had, and one of the greatest individual feats in baseball history.

In the very first inning of that night game, with two out, Stan caught hold of a Preacher Roe fast ball and drove it out of the ball park into Bedford Avenue for a home run, and St. Louis wasn't to be headed. Stan got himself another hit off Roe, two out of three for the game, and the Redbirds romped off the field victorious, 3–1. The Dodger lead was cut to one and one-half.

The next day, with Brooklyn leading 4–3 in the ninth inning, Erv Palica walked Stan who promptly stole second and came dashing into Roy Campanella at home plate for the tying run on Marty Marion's infield single.

The Cards went on to win the game, 5–4, and they were just half a game away from the top rung in the ladder.

In the next game Stan really went to work, belting Don Newcombe, Paul Minner and Carl Erskine for a single, a double, a triple and a homer. Only a great running catch, deep against the center field wall, stopped Stan for another five for five day. Thirty-four thousand screaming fans saw the one-man onslaught, and St. Louis was out in front of the National League race for the first time that season.

The fans who jammed the stands at Ebbets Feld came to cheer their Dodgers on to victory and back into first place. But it was Stan Musial who drew the first big ovation of the game. Stan was "the Man" in Brooklyn, the most dangerous single threat against the pennant hopes of the Brooklyn ball club, but the slugging Donora Greyhound had found a place in the heart of Flatbush-ro

"Hit it, Stan!" they dared him.

In the very first inning of that all-important game, t is exactly what Stan did. With Lou Klein on base by w of a walk, Musial blasted a triple off the center field wall on Ralph Branca's first pitch, and the Cardinals were ahead, 1–0.

The lead didn't last long, however, as the Dodgers answered back, driving four big runs across the plate. The Brooklyn fans hollered their heads off with victory looming large, and with that victory, first place in the National League again.

Branca was pitching good ball, too. After that first inning triple of Musial's, he had been able to still the Redbird bats to a whisper. His fast ball was hopping. In the sixth inning the Dodger hurler got both Red Schoendienst and Lou Klein swinging for that third strike. Then up stepped Stan and the fans let out with a "Oooooh, that Man!"

Musial took a strike, then a ball. The next pitch was a fast one, a little low and a little to the outside, and Stan whacked it on a line against the right center field concrete for a slashing double.

Stan had a way of starting that two-out rally for the Cards. This time the boys kept to the script. Slaughter followed with a walk. Ron Northey and Glen Nelson contributed a couple of doubles and the score was tied at 4–4.

That was the way the game ended, 4–4. The Dodgers had to make a train for Chicago and St. Louis left for Philadelphia. The Cardinals were in first place by half game.

e slimmest kind of lead, but the Redbirds be-
and sing pennant. Mostly it was sing.

Weaver, the club trainer, had an old phonograph in 1942, when St. Louis came up with the National League pennant. "Pass the Biscuits, Mirandy" was the record they kept playing on it.

"Keep that record going, boy," Doc Weaver had admonished, "and we win the flag."

They played it till it was worn down, then replaced it with another "Pass the Biscuits, Mirandy" until they clinched the league championship.

"It worked!" yelled Doc Weaver. "I told you it would work! Works every time!"

The boys howled with glee and they believed every word Doc Weaver said. They did have the pennant, didn't they?

"Pass the Biscuits, Mirandy" worked in 1946, too, the

year the Redbirds tied with the Dodgers for the flag, then went on to beat them in the play-off.

In 1949 they had a new phonograph, but they weren't decided on the right disk. They couldn't get hold of another "Pass the Biscuits, Mirandy," and the boys were having a time finding a substitute.

"Make it 'Ah! Sweet Mystery of Life'!" urged Red Schoendienst.

"Make it 'I Pass the Graveyard at Midnight,'" said Lanier. "Play that on the loudspeaker and I'll pitch you a no-hit game every time."

"Boogie-woogie," said Stan Musial. He liked jazz, but good jazz.

"How about a little Beethoven?" offered Howie Pollet, who liked the more serious music.

Meanwhile Doc Weaver kept scouring the record shops for "Pass the Biscuits, Mirandy," and the Redbirds kept slugging away for the pennant.

Stan had had one of his most terrific series in those four days in Ebbets Field. He had been up at bat fifteen times, whacked out nine hits, two doubles, two triples and two home runs, scored seven times. He had come to Brooklyn with a batting average of .291. He left Brooklyn, after batting for an unbelievable .600, with an average of .304.

In Philadelphia Musial continued his one-man rampage that had lifted his batting average past the .300 mark. His inspired play set fire to the rest of the Cardinals. In the first game of the series Stan drove out two doubles and a single, hammering three runs across the plate for St. Louis. In the next game, in addition to his regular cluster of safe hits, with the bases full of Redbirds, he smashed a double off the center field wall to drive three St. Louis runs across the plate.

With Stan Musial wielding the most destructive bat in the league, St. Louis stayed on top. By August 24 the Man was hitting the ball at a .324 clip, second only to league-leading Jackie Robinson. The Redbirds were Number One in the race for the flag.

That was the way it was until the last days in September. Then, maybe it was because Doc Weaver never found that "Pass the Biscuits, Mirandy" record, St. Louis faltered. Stan kept to his torrid pace, built up his batting average to .338, but it wasn't enough. The Cardinals dropped four of their last five games, and the pennant went to their arch rivals the Brooklyn Dodgers.

"They've done a swell job," the sport scribes wrote of Eddie Dyer and the ball club. "They've come in first or second in the race for nine years running. That's a great record—one that they can be proud of." As a matter of fact, Eddie had almost won the pennant three years in a row. But a miss is as good as a mile and Eddie wasn't consoled by the applause of the writers.

Nor was Stan too happy about his .338 average. He had finished just four points behind Robinson.

"If I hadn't gone for that home run in April and May, I might have been on top. It's all my fault that we lost the pennant. I should never have tried for the home run crown, should have played my regular game."

But no one else found fault with the slugging Redbird. No one could. For his 1949 batting record, Stan showed two hundred and seven safe base hits, more than anyone else in the league. He drove out forty-one doubles to lead the league in that department again. He walloped thirteen triples, league leader there, too. He belted thirty-six home runs—without trying, this time. He drove in one hundred twenty-three runs for St. Louis and scored another one hundred twenty-eight.

Only Stan Musial could remain dissatisfied with this kind of slugging. He meant to do better. He meant to regain that batting championship and help his club win the pennant.

CHAPTER 22

Stan Musial began to whack the ball at a prodigious clip right from the very beginning in the 1950 baseball season. He hit safely in the first twenty-three games of the schedule, except one, during which he piled up a fifteen-game winning streak. That streak was just an indication of what was to come.

On June 20th, with more than twenty-seven thousand shouting fans jamming the Polo Grounds, Stan Musial blasted Sheldon Jones for a terrific drive into the stands to overcome an early Giant lead. More important than that, it was Stan's fifteen hundredth hit as a major-leaguer.

The fans rose in a great ovation to the slugger, as the announcement came loud over the loud-speakers, and Stan modestly doffed his cap as he crossed home plate.

"That's a great record, Stan!" shouted Red Schoendienst, as the big St. Louis batter came into the dugout.

"Thanks," said Stan, but that fifteen hundred-hit mark wasn't enough. He wanted to get into that select group of big-league hitters who had hit over two thousand hits in the big time—Ty Cobb, Rogers Hornsby, Paul and Lloyd Waner, Joe DiMaggio.

Marty Marion didn't have to be told. He knew what Stan was thinking.

"Two thousand next stop!" he hollered back at Musial, and Stan just grinned, but he lost no time in going after that cherished mark.

The very next day, June 21st, Musial cracked out two

hits and scored three runs in a 14–6 rout of the New York club.

An interesting item, though few recognized it as such that day, was the announcement by the Giants' front office that it had signed a young Negro ballplayer in Fairfield, Alabama, and that they had farmed him out to their Trenton ball club. That youngster, just nineteen years old, was Willie Mays. Not one of the thirty thousand fans in the Polo Grounds that afternoon had ever heard of Willie Mays. Nor had any one of the players on the field. But Willie Mays was to come up in short order to challenge the Donora Greyhound's supremacy in the league.

But it was all Stan Musial in 1950. On June 26th he beat out two hits in four to beat the Boston Braves in a ten-inning struggle, 7–6. That date was memorable. It was the beginning of one of the longest hitting streaks in major league history.

On the 27th Stan hit a home run to beat the Cubs in the first game of a double-header, 3–2. In the nightcap Musial banged out three more hits to lead the Cards to a sweep of both games, 4–1.

It was the same game after game. Stan kept hitting them where no one could field them. On July 15th his big bat crushed the league-leading Philadelphia team, but it was a costly win. Stan came limping into the dugout after sliding into third base, "Hey, Doc, I think I twisted my knee on that play. Better look it over."

Doc Weaver carefully examined the battered knee. "Looks like a bad wrench. It's swelling up."

All the St. Louis players were standing around him.

"You're not hurt?"

"Nothing serious, Stan?"

Every Cardinal, from manager Eddie Dyer to the bat boy, knew what Stan meant to the club.

"You don't have to make every single a double!" scowled Eddie.

Stan grinned through his pain. He knew that Dyer was just letting off steam, that he was really worried.

"It's just a wrench," offered the Donora Greyhound. "Let me get upon my feet."

Doc Weaver yelled, "No! Keep off your feet."

It was too late.

Stan was up, trying to move about, but he grimaced with pain.

"Here!" hollered Doc Weaver. "Help me get him back into the clubhouse.

The Cardinals won that game, 4–2, cutting the Phillies' lead to just one game, but there was no joy among the Redbirds after the game.

In the clubhouse the players crowded around Musial. They looked at his knee all taped up. They were too glum to talk.

"How bad is it?" demanded Eddie Dyer.

"Bad enough to keep him on the bench for a couple of weeks," said Doc Weaver. "No games for at least ten days, and a complete rest."

"I'm playing tomorrow!" contradicted Stan Musial.

"If Doc says you're out for a couple of weeks," growled the Cardinal skipper, "then you're out two weeks!"

"I'm playing tomorrow," insisted Musial.

"Not if I can help it," announced Doc Weaver.

"I'm playing!"

Stan was adamant.

Eddie Dyer just shook his head. The next day Stan was out on the field. He could barely hobble around, yet he played an amazing game to lead the Cardinals to an 8–6 victory over Philadelphia, a victory that enabled the Cardinals to move into a tie for first place.

A week later, against the Giants, Stan belted the New Yorkers for two doubles in the first game of a double-header, hit again and scored two runs in the second, moving the Cards one game in front of the second-place Phillies. Musial's batting streak had run to twenty-three straight, and he was still playing with a taped up and badly wrenched knee.

On the 21st of July Musial belted two singles and a tremendous line-drive home run to whip Sal Maglie and Durocher's Giants. On the 22nd he whacked two homers and a double, three for five, to beat the Braves in the first of two, 8–5. In the second game he belted out two more homers for an 11–7 win. That streak was riding.

On July 25th, against Preacher Roe and the Dodgers, Stan, the Man, larruped out a single, a double and another home run.

On July 26th the Donora Greyhound banged out another two safeties against the Brooklyn club.

On that first hit of the 26th of July, 1950, the Ebbets Field loud-speakers had a special announcement for the jam-packed park.

"Stan Musial has now hit safely in thirty games straight. He has tied a National League record for hitting in consecutive games. Only ten men have done this before in National League history. Stan Musial makes it eleven!"

The Flatbush fans gave him a great ovation.

"That's hitting them, Stan!"

"What a man! That's Stan, the Man!"

Stan was pleased at matching a great baseball record.

He would have liked to reach Rogers Hornsby's mark of hitting safely in thirty-three straight games, then gone on to meet Tommy Holmes's record of thirty-seven games in a row. Then there was that old-timer Willie Keeler's sensational forty-four-game-straight hitting streak and finally the unbelievable fifty-six consecutive game-hitting streak of Joe DiMaggio's. But Stan, unhappily, had to settle with the simpler glory of the thirty-game record, when Joe Hatten, Rex Barney and Billy Loes combined to stop the slugger on July 27th.

The Donora Greyhound was stopped in that thirty-first game, but only temporarily. The very next day, he drove out a double and a single to spark an 8–3 win over the Giants. By the middle of August he was leading the league in batting with a prodigious average of .361, seventeen points ahead of his nearest rival, the winner of the 1949 batting crown Jackie Robinson.

Unfortunately, the St. Louis Cardinals couldn't keep pace with their slugger. Despite Stan's brilliant individual efforts, the Cardinals couldn't keep up the fast pace. Game after game was lost by the narrowest margin.

One afternoon, after a galling, one-run ninth inning defeat, Musial called the team together for an emergency meeting. "Men," he said, "I've got Manager Dyer's permission for this meeting. I just want to see if we can work this one-run jinx out. I want your ideas. Why are we losing these close ball games, when we ought to be up in first place? Red? Marty? Any ideas?"

Red Schoendienst spoke up. "Stan I know all the players are doing their level best."

"I know that," snapped Musial. "I know that we're going all out to win, but that isn't enough. We're falling behind every day. We'll be lucky to finish in the first division if we keep to this pace."

"Stan, I'm sure I speak for all the players," said Marty Marion. "It's a tough thing to try to analyze why we're losing all these close games. You know that we're not getting the kind of young replacements that this team needs. But I know that we can certainly go out there tomorrow and give it the old college try. I know that we can do a lot better."

The spirit of the team was willing, but the talent was no longer up to that of the Cardinals of former years. The team played their hearts out. Musial, Marty Marion and Red Schoendienst played superhuman ball, but that wasn't enough. The aging ball club fell apart as Philadelphia, Boston, Brooklyn and the Giants swept past the Cardinals in the final league standings. Stan Musial was the only bright spot in the whole 1950 season for the St. Louis club.

For a while Jackie Robinson challenged the Donora Greyhound for the batting title, but Stan pulled way out in front. He finished his schedule with the superb average of .346. Jackie Robinson, second leading batter, trailed him by a big eighteen points. Duke Snider was third, twenty-five points behind the St. Louis slugger. Stan, the Man was batting king in the National League again, and for the fourth time in his eight years of big-league ball.

His record for the 1950 schedule reads: one hundred ninety-two hits, forty-one doubles, seven triples and twenty-eight big home runs. He drove in one hundred nine runs, the third year straight, the fourth time in five years that he had batted in more than one hundred runs for his ball club. Altogether he scored one hundred five runs for St. Louis. Except in his first year as a Cardinal,

Stan had scored more than one hundred runs in every season he had played.

The year 1950 was another remarkable season for the Donora sensation. He proved beyond a doubt that he was entitled to recognition as one of the stalwart all-time stars of the game. There were more great seasons, more records to smash for the St. Louis Cardinals one-man team Stan Musial.

CHAPTER 23

The St. Louis Cardinals had dropped to fifth place in the final standings of the 1950 National League schedule. It was the poorest finish for the Redbirds in twelve years. For the first time in nine years, they had completely dropped out of the fight for the flag. For the first time in nine years they had not finished first or second in their circuit. It was a foregone conclusion that there were going to be some changes made on the St. Louis club and that the first man to go would be their manager Eddie Dyer, the man who had won the pennant four years in a row for the Cardinals and finished in second place.

"When anything goes wrong with a ball club, they always get the manager first," said Stan Musial. "The manager is important enough, but what about the rest of the ball club? We've gotten older," continued Stan. "We've gotten slower on our feet. We need some top-notch young players, and we'll move right to the top again. Young, hustling ball players are what we need."

"You slowing up, too?" they asked Musial.

"I can't beat out as many infield hits as I used to," answered Stan. "Sure, I'm getting older. I'll be thirty-one this November. We ballplayers get old fast."

"You'll never get old," responded the writer, talking with the St. Louis star. "Not the way you've been walloping the ball. You're good for ten more years."

"Sounds good," replied the thoughtful Musial, "but that's all. We all slow down sooner or later. I don't see how they can blame a manager of a ball club for that."

Stan was essentially right in his thinking, but that didn't change the situation. Eddie Dyer had brought home a fifth-place club in 1950 and he was scheduled to be replaced by the St. Louis front office. The news came to Musial as he was plying his off-season trade, being the host in Stan Musial's and Biggie's Steak House in St. Louis.

"They've just fired Eddie Dyer," announced Biggie, producing the item in the sports page, and the usually calm Musial hit the ceiling.

"Yes, and that's going to give St. Louis the pennant!" he snapped sarcastically.

"Maybe it will," offered Biggie, placatingly.

Stan didn't hear him.

"Eddie Dyer is one of the best pilots in baseball," he shouted. "He is better than that. He is one of the swellest fellows in the game. I like Eddie Dyer."

"You like Marty Marion, too," offered his restaurateur partner. "He's a smart ballplayer."

"Sure," agreed Stan, softening for a moment.

Marty Marion had been signed to manage the Cards in 1951. Marty had played ball, right alongside of Stan, for more than eight years. Stan respected Marion both as a man and as a ballplayer. He counted Marion among his best friends.

"Sure, I like Marion," he said. "He'll make a great manager. They just had no right to fire Dyer. It just doesn't figure."

"You didn't want the job yourself, Stan?"

Musial did a double-take.

"Me? Manager?" he queried.

"You. Manager," repeated Biggie.

Slowly a big grin spread over Stan's handsome face.

"You might have had something, Biggie," he said. "I guess I would like that a lot. Yes sir, one of these days I might like it very much."

"Every ballplayer wants to be manager somedy. You're no different, are you, Stan?"

"I guess not," answered Musial thoughtfully. "Sure, I'd like to pilot a club sometime. Not now! I've still got a few years of good baseball playing in me. There's plenty of time to think about managing a ball club."

"That's what I thought," said Biggie. "I just wanted to hear you say it."

"Well, I said it," responded Musial, and he was scowling again. "But that's got nothing to do with the way the front office kicked out Eddie Dyer."

"Nothing you can do about it," offered Biggie.

"Sure," assented Stan, "but Eddie could play me in left field, center field or first base. It didn't matter. I'd play anywhere for Eddie Dyer. Next year I'm through being shoved around. I'll play the field or first base, but not both. Marion will have to decide. I just don't like what they've done to Eddie Dyer!"

Stan had a little time to cool off between seasons. In February, 1951, at the request of the War Department, he went overseas to Germany to entertain our Army of Occupation there. With him were Jim Konstanty, the relief pitcher who had hurled Philadelphia to its first pennant in ages, the Most Valuable Player of the year. Frankie Frisch, Cub manager, Charley Grimm, manager of the Boston Braves, and National League umpire Larry Goetz. They talked a lot of baseball and Stan had a lot of time to think about the changing status of the St. Louis Cards, but he had made up his mind about his status. He would play one position, and one position only, under Marty Marion.

There were a number of changes in the St. Louis line-up that year. Peanuts Lowrey was playing the outfield. So was Chuck Diering. Nippy Jones was at first base. Emil Rojek was at shortstop. Cloyd Boyer and Tom Poholsky had come up from Rochester. Joe Presko had come up from Houston. There were still Enos Slaughter, Red Schoendienst, Del Rice and Max Lanier, but little else to remind Stan of the club he had joined in 1941. It was an untried, untested ball club. It was going to meet with some tough sledding ahead, and Stan, at the beginning of that 1951 season, wasn't going to be too much help.

All through April and May Musial batted around the .250 mark. He just couldn't get going. In the first week of June he drove out seven hits in two games against the Giants, four hits on June third, including two prodigious home runs, two more home runs and a single the next day. Stan was batting an anemic .251, however, as the clubs passed the middle of June.

Mail from the fans was heavy.

"Tape your eyes when you go to bed at night. That should sharpen your batting eye," offered a worried fan.

"You're crowding the plate too much," wrote another. "Step back a bit and we'll be cheering you every time you come up to the plate."

"You've been swinging too late," suggested another ad-mirer of the St. Louis star. "You're getting too anxious. Slow down a bit. It'll pay off in hits."

The baseball fans were really worried. Stan was irri-tated with himself.

"I want to hit them for you," he said to Marion, hoping that the new Cardinal pilot wasn't getting any wrong ideas.

"You'll get there, Stan," came back Marty Marion, anticipating Stan's concern. "You've started slow before," he added. "You'll come up fast."

Musial came up fast, all right, faster than even Marion had hoped.

On the morning of June 17th Stan ordered himself a long practice batting session. He worked in that batting cage for more than four hours. That night he doubled off Brooklyn pitcher Ben Wade and got his first lusty hit in weeks. It was the beginning of one of the most sensational hitting surges in baseball history.

From June 17th to June 27th Stan was unstoppable. In that ten day stretch he played in twelve games, went to bat forty-three times and belted out twenty-four hits, ten doubles, four home runs and batted in seventeen runs. In those ten days Stan batted at a .558 pace, and his booming bat zoomed the Cardinals to a new high.

Even more remarkable was that seven-day stretch from June 21st to June 27th. In that brief week, and against such pitching aces as Sal Maglie, Jim Hearn, Robin Roberts, Dave Koslo, Murry Dickson and Johnny Lindell, the mighty Donora Greyhound banged out nineteen hits in twenty-seven times at bat for the blazing batting average of .704! And among those nineteen hits were six doubles and four home runs.

The Redbirds spurted, of course, but Marty Marion wasn't fighting for the pennant that year. He had a young club. He was aiming for first division and Musial's bat was going to insure it.

"Great going, Stan," he said, slapping his slugger on the back as he trotted back into the dugout.

Stan smiled at his skipper. There had been that quiet tension between them, right from the beginning of the 1951 season, mainly because of the firing of Eddie Dyer, but never an unfriendliness. On the contrary, Musial always went all-out for his club, and for Marion as well.

Earlier, in May, the Cardinals had been hit hard by a flu bug. It sent the Redbirds into a protracted losing streak, salvaged only by an occasional win. St. Louis was moving down toward the cellar of the league. Then Stan was stricken by the same flu germ and the Cardinals, playing without their slugger, lost five straight.

They were two runs behind in the eighth inning of what promised to be their sixth straight defeat. There were two men on base but two men were out and the pitcher was scheduled to hit. Marty Marion looked around the bench for a pinch hitter. Stan, still weak, still wracked with the fever, caught his manager's eye.

"Want me to hit, Marty?" he asked.

Marion was desperate but he didn't see how he could send a wan and shivering Stan Musial up to the plate, especially against the ace Cincinnati hurler Herman Wehmeier.

"Let me get up there," said Stan. "Let me take a swing at the ball. I think I can belt one, Marty."

Marion hesitated a moment. Musial was still the best man he had on his club.

"Go ahead," he said.

Luke Sewell, Redleg manager, looked twice to make sure, as Musial slowly walked up to home plate. He just couldn't believe it.

Wehmeier, who ordinarily might have been a little worried by the appearance of Stan at the plate, was all confidence as he looked down at the ailing man. He pitched two quick strikes on Stan. He came down to his stop position, fired what should have been the third strike and the end of the St. Louis threat. It wasn't. Stan swung with all the strength he had in his weakened body, drove the ball hard, smashed it over the right field fence for a three-run homer—and the ball game.

Marty Marion will never forget that clutch performance. It helped bridge the gulf which had come between the two baseball men. In August that bridge was completed.

St. Louis was still fighting to make that first division berth and there were just two months left in the season. Solly Hemus had come up to play a great game at shortstop for the Redbirds, but first base was still the club's big weakness, and Stan, true to his promise, had stuck to playing the one position, the outfield. Marty knew well enough about Stan's resolve to stay in that one spot in the Card defenses, but he was in a spot, and he decided to move.

"We need you on first base," he said to Stan, putting the proposition right on the line. "If we're going anywhere at all this year, we need you on first base. How about it, Stan? For the good of the team."

Stan smiled. He shook Marty's hand. He played first base. The St. Louis Cardinals began to move at a phenomenal clip.

The New York Giants were the big club during the final stages of the 1951 season. But St. Louis was just a shade behind in its great August and September streak. With Stan smashing the ball, the Cardinals swept into third place with twenty-three victories in their last thirty-two games.

"Stan did it," said Marty Marion. "His bat and his team play. He is the greatest team player in the league."

They were comparing him, with all the facts and figures, with the greatest batters in the history of baseball.

THE GREATEST LEFT-HANDED HITTER IN THE HISTORY OF THE GAME

So read the twelve-inch heading on a sports story on Stan.

When all the tabulation for the season was over, they trotted out the numbers to show that Stan's record was a shade better than Ted Williams'. Stan's lifetime average to date was .3473. Ted Williams' comparable record showed an average of .3466. There was a difference of seven tenths of a point in Musial's favor.

His batting average for the year had been a brilliant .355. He had clouted out two hundred five hits, thirty doubles, twelve triples, thirty-two home runs. He had batted in one hundred eight runs, scored one hundred twenty-four. He was the leader in the runs scored department for the third time in his career. He led in triples for the fifth time and tied Sam Crawford for the league record for leading in triples. He was, of course, the league-leading hitter for 1951. This was the second year straight he had won that crown, the fifth time since coming up to the big leagues.

The year 1951 was one of Stan's greatest and the *Sporting News,* for the second time, honored Stan Musial as Major League Player of the year.

CHAPTER 24

A manager's job is the most insecure job in baseball. In 1950 Eddie Dyer had piloted the St. Louis Cardinals. In 1951 it had been Marty Marion. When Stan Musial reported for spring training in 1952, there was a new manager for the St. Louis Redbirds—Eddie Stanky, one of the most colorful men in the game.

Stanky was a scrappy player, a throwback to the swashbuckling Gas House Gang of St. Louis. He was in the game to the last second of it, fighting for victory until the last man was out.

They called him the "Brat." He had sparked Brooklyn, Boston and New York to pennants. Wherever he played he infused his teammates with the will to win. He was no great slugger. He had hit for a .300 average only twice in his playing career—.320 with Boston, a flat .300 with New York—but he was a smart baseball man and commanded the respect of all his players. Eddie Stanky was a great team player. So was Stan Musial. They were destined to get along.

St. Louis got off to a slow start, winning only seven of their first sixteen games, but Stan started winging right off with the first cry of "Play ball!" By the first week in May the slugger was batting .349. He had belted out thirteen hits in his last twenty-four times at bat. By the middle of July Stan was whacking the ball for a .394 average. The Donora Greyhound, who hadn't missed an All-Star game since his first year in the major leagues, was the top vote getter for the 1952 classic. He had just completed another great batting streak which had run through twenty-four games in which Musial had belted thirty-six hits, three doubles, three triples and four homers among them. He was still Stan, the Man, and he gave quick notice that he was after that batting crown for the third year in a row.

"How do you do it?" the sport scribes wanted to know. "Is it the way you stand in the box, coiled up like a serpent, and then whip that bat across the plate? How did you get that stance in the first place?"

Stan, always modest about his own prowess, grinned.

"I guess it's just natural with me," he said. "The truth is that I never saw anyone else bat that way."

"Didn't anyone ever try to get you to change that stance?"

Stan was still grinning. Who would ever want to change the batting stance of a man who hammered the ball the way he did.

"I know it's unnatural," he said, "but I like it. I feel comfortable. I think it gives me more power, too. I bring my whole body into my swing."

"You change your style sometimes, don't you?" queried the sports writers.

"Sometimes. In some parks I aim for the short right field fence. I pull the ball more in the Polo Grounds."

But Polo Grounds or Ebbets Field, against the Phillies or the Cubs, against every team in the league, it didn't matter which, the Donora Greyhound continued his great slugging.

At a Chamber of Commerce dinner in St. Louis, honoring Musial, Giles got up to speak and the president of the National League said, simply and honestly, "Stan Musial is the greatest player of all time."

Will Harridge, president of the American League, got up at the same dinner to pay his own tribute to the Cardinal star.

"There may have been better hitters," he said, "and there may have been better fielders, but baseball history will chronicle Musial as one of the greatest players of all time."

Both presidents of the major leagues were agreed on one point, the greatness of Stan Musial.

Manager Eddie Stanky, the Brat, didn't go all the way, but he made his own good speech, introducing Stan as the next speaker at that dinner.

"Now I come to a fellow who needs no introduction," began the new Cardinal pilot. "He's the greatest player in the game today, a manager's delight, a willing worker, a fellow who signs everything—in fact, he does everything but talk. I don't see how he gets away without being asked to speak."

Eddie had a big, mischievous grin on his face.

"Anyway," he continued, "I give you Stan, the Man, Musial!"

Musial, blushing to his roots, got up, all right, but not to speak. He was down in his seat as quickly as he had stood up.

Stanky just looked at Musial in frank approval, as the applause swelled the dining hall.

"Is that all?" he yelled at his star player. "Just up and down and nothing else?"

It was good for a laugh and Eddie liked to get that laughter. More than that, it showed Stan for what he was, a man who had not allowed his remarkably great career on the diamond to swell his head, or change one note in his genuinely honest make-up.

St. Louis wasn't in the fight for the pennant that year; they were in the midst of a tough battle for second place, and Stan's big bat was with them all the way.

In eight games through Labor Day, Stan banged out sixteen hits. He drove out nine for sixteen in two games with Pittsburgh. He was batting at .337, twenty-one points ahead of his nearest rival for the batting crown, big Ted Kluszewski of the Cincinnati Redlegs.

On September 9th, in Philadelphia, the loud-speakers blared again for the Donora Greyhound.

Curt Simmons, Philadelphia ace, was pitching. It was the fourth inning and Stan came to bat and promptly lined a sharp single into center field. The big speakers got under way.

"Stan Musial has just delivered his two thousandth hit!" The Philadelphia fans, who would battle to prove that their admiration of the Man was as great as anyone else's, rose in a tremendous ovation.

"There have been ninety major-leaguers who have collected two thousand hits or more in the history of the game since 1876, but Stan Musial is the only active player in baseball to have made that mark!"

The game was no longer important. This was Stan Musial's day, and the fans let him hear it!

Stan came home with that batting title in 1952. It was his third straight batting crown and that was a record. He was the first left-handed batter to lead the league in hitting for three consecutive seasons in all the seventy-seven years of baseball history. And he was right up there with the greatest right-hand hitters, too.

This was Stan's sixth batting title in his ten-year career as a major-leaguer. He was only one behind the Hall of Fame Rogers Hornsby, just two behind the immortal

Honus Wagner's all-time record of eight batting crowns.

In all, Stan set three records in 1952. He had scored one hundred or more runs per season for nine consecutive seasons. He led in base hits for six seasons. His lifetime slugging percentage, for ten years or more, was .579.

Of all the active major-leaguers who had been to bat one thousand times or more, Stan led the pack with a mark of .346 for that long stretch. His nearest rival twenty-four points behind, was Jackie Robinson of the Brooklyn Dodgers. Dale Mitchell of the Indians was next with a .317 average. Then came Johnny Mize, Bill McCosky of the Indians, George Kell, Bill Goodman of the Red Sox, and just seven more.

There was one man on the inactive list—Ted Williams. If he were playing, he should have edged Stan Musial, but by something just less than a whisker.

Ted Williams' batting average for his baseball lifetime, at the end of 1952, was .34674. Stan's average was .34617. The difference between them was .00057. That's about one more hit in two thousand times at bat. That's how closely both these great sluggers were matched.

But Ted Williams wasn't playing ball in 1952 and Grantland Rice, the dean of all sports writers, wrote with great feeling, "With the departure of Joe DiMaggio and Ted Williams, Stan Musial is the only diamond brilliant left for most fans to follow."

This was a statement which was going to be echoed in the season of 1953.

CHAPTER 25

Grantland Rice called Stan Musial "the only diamond brilliant" left in baseball. That was the mildest statement on record, compared with the statement Ty Cobb, Number One man in Baseball's Hall of Fame, was to make shortly afterward. In a signed article for a national magazine, the all-time great ballplayer blasted away at the modern game and practically everyone and everything connected with it. He found praise for Ty Cobb and Phil Rizzuto and for practically nobody else. The statement set off a sizable storm in the baseball world and the winter hot-stove league had more than enough to talk about before the 1953 season opened.

"No man has ever been a perfect ballplayer," said Ty Cobb. "Stan Musial, however, is the closest to being perfect in the game today. I've seen greater hitters and greater runners and greater fielders, but he puts them all together like no one else, except the way George Sisler did. He's certainly one of the greatest players of all time. In my book, he's a better player than Joe DiMaggio was in his prime."

The sport scribes were quick to draw Stan's attention to Ty Cobb's adulation.

"What do you say about it, Stan?"

Stan blushed, but he was more than embarrassed, he was on the spot.

"I don't want to argue with Ty Cobb," he said. "Cobb is baseball's greatest. I don't want to contradict him, but I can't say that I was ever as good as Joe DiMaggio."

Stan shook his head in disbelief.

"No," he continued. "I don't think there was ever a day when I could reach Joe DiMaggio, when Joe was in his top form. That DiMaggio was the best, the greatest ballplayer I ever saw on any diamond anywhere."

There were a number of fans who wouldn't go along with Stan's statement either.

"Musial is a greater team player."

"Musial plays for the club."

"He's an all-out man all the way down through the ninth inning."

Ty Cobb said that, too.

"Stan Musial will score from first on a single. You don't see much of that kind of running around today. He plays as hard when his club is away out in front in a game, as he does when they're just a run or two behind. He'll go after a ball, even in an exhibition game, diving for a shoestring catch, as if the World Series depended on it. He's my kind of ballplayer."

That wasn't all Cobb had to say about Musial. He pointed up the Cardinal's versatility.

"He plays anywhere you put him, left field, center field. Didn't he win the Most Valuable Player Award, playing first base?"

Nobody could argue against Cobb on this statement.

"He has the power of Napoleon Lajoie," said Ty Cobb, comparing him to the Hall of Fame old-timer. "He has the stamina of Eddie Collins," went on Ty Cobb, recalling all the greats of another year. "He is as steady as old Honus Wagner."

This was the greatest kind of praise from the man who has been called baseball's all-time greatest player. It might have gone to any ordinary ballplayer's head. Not Stan's.

He was not especially happy about Cobb's statements.

"Is that me he's talking about?"

He was apologetic, modest as always.

"That's all very nice for Ty Cobb to say all those things about me but I think he's off base this time."

That was what Stan said, and he believed it, but it put pressure on him anyway, when he got down to spring training in 1953.

"How do you do it, Stan?"

"Show us, Musial."

The rookies always did come to Stan to get pointers in spring training. They came to him more eagerly and more insistently this year.

"You just get up there and meet the ball," Stan advised them.

He had always been happy to help the younger ballplayers. He had even been eager to help them. This year there was something extra added. Ty Cobb's articles.

"I don't know how to tell you this exactly," Stan tried to explain. "Back in 1948—that was my biggest year—I could just about guess what the pitchers were going to throw me. I seemed to sense when they were sending me a fast ball, a curve, a change of pace. I was ready for it."

"What do you do now, Stan?" asked an earnest rookie.

Stan looked at the youngster, and the rookie was as serious as the Man himself.

"I just get up there," resumed Musial after a moment, "and I expect they'll send me a fast ball. I wait for it. Then I take my cut at it."

"As easy as that?" questioned a completely awed youngster.

It seemed that easy in spring training and in the exhibition games as Stan began to whack the cover off the ball and made Ty Cobb's tribute stand up.

But once the schedule of the regular season got under way, Stan fell into that annual April slump. He was still in the slump at the beginning of June, hitting at a miserable .220.

Eddie Stanky paced the dugout, spent sleepless nights, as the Cardinals slipped further and further down in the National League standings, knowing that the one man to stop the debacle, the one man to start the club climbing back, was Stan Musial.

"How about it, Stan!" he yelled to the slugger up at bat.

"Get a hit, Stan!"

He was pleading, not demanding. Stan was in there trying, all right. He just wasn't getting a good piece of the ball. His timing was off. He was tense and cutting at bad pitches.

"I don't know what's wrong."

Stan shook his head. So did Eddie Stanky.

"I guess I'll have to be working out a bit more in that batting cage," offered the Man.

"You'll come around," said Eddie.

Stan went for that batting cage, and though it took him a little longer this year, he began to hit again, the way he always hit, the way the fans, and Ty Cobb, too, expected him to hit.

Two for three against the Giants. Eight out of ten against the Dodgers in a tough double-header. He walloped the pitching of the Milwaukee Braves and Cincinnati Reds and the Chicago Cubs. He began to drive out those sharp doubles. He was hitting the home run ball more often. By the middle of July he was up there again, where he belonged, among the big .300 hitters.

"Attaboy, Stan!"

"That's hitting them, Musial!"

"Oooooh! Stan, the Man!"

The Donora Greyhound was hitting .251 on July 17th. The Cards had played fifty-six of their one hundred fifty-four-game schedule. For the rest of the schedule, however, Musial's bat was the most powerful in the league, batting at a tremendous clip of .381.

He hit safely in twenty-nine of the last thirty-one games, batting at a sensational clip of .437. In the last fifteen games of the schedule, Stan hammered the ball for the unbelievable average of .468. He had started slowly, as he had done before. He had come up again fast, as he had done before. But this time he started back up too late and Carl Furillo of the Brooklyn Dodgers nosed him out of what might have been his seventh batting crown by a meager five points.

The year had started with the tremendous publicity, to Stan's keen embarrassment. He hadn't asked for the big build-up Ty Cobb had given him, and even though the fans were, for the most part, in agreement with Cobb that Stan merited everything that was said about his greatness, it put undue pressure on the slugger. He just couldn't unwind. When he did, however, it was with all his former power. Although Stan didn't win the batting crown, for his eleventh season straight, continuing right from where he had started in the major leagues, the Man had come in with a better than .300 batting mark.

This year it was .337, actually a point better than his 1952 mark. He drove out two hundred hits, the sixth year he had collected two hundred or more safeties. He banged out fifty-three doubles, the most doubles in his career, and again, for the seventh time the leader in that department of slugging. He drove out nine triples and thirty big home runs. He batted in one hundred thirteen St. Louis runs and scored one hundred twenty-seven.

Stan tied one baseball record and set another in 1953. For the sixth consecutive season he had belted the ball for a total of more than three hundred bases. This feat equaled the mark of Joe Medwick, who had turned the trick in 1934–1939. Stan, too, with his three hundred sixty-one total base mark for the season, had made it nine seasons of three hundred or more total bases for him. This broke the long-standing record of Rogers Hornsby, who had collected eight of them in his great playing years.

CHAPTER 26

More than twenty-six thousand fans jammed the St. Louis ball park on May 2, 1954, to see the Cardinals and the New York Giants clash in an early season double-header. This was a big crowd for any baseball game in the Mound City. It was an unusually large crowd for a spring battle. It was to prove a fitting crowd for one of the greatest, most spectacular days in the history of the national game.

The Giants had come into town with its sensational pitching stars, Sal Maglie, Johnny Antonelli, Jim Hearn, Larry Jansen, Don Liddle, Hoyt Wilhelm, and with the amazing Willie Mays. These weren't the men, however, who were to provide the great baseball drama of the day.

Eddie Stanky had practically cleaned house on the Redbird roster. He wanted to have a young team on the field, a club which wouldn't win the pennant in 1954 but which would build quickly into a pennant contender. Enos Slaughter had been traded to the New York Yankees and there were two new faces in the Cardinal outfield—Wally Moon and Rip Repulski. Tommy Alston, a young Negro player, was at first base. Grammas was at shortstop, Ray Jablonski at third. But it wasn't any of these rookies who was going to electrify jam-packed Busch Stadium that day.

It was the thirty-three-year-old Stan Musial, the Man himself, who was going to stand the park on end, who was going to have the fans up in their seats, cheering and hollering for more than five and a half hours straight.

It all started quietly enough. Johnny Antonelli walked

Stan the first time Musial came to bat, and the crowd hollered loud enough when the Man came in to score. There was nothing to indicate that this was going to be a day baseball could never forget.

In the third inning, with Antonelli still in the box, Musial caught hold of a low pitch and belted it deep and over the roof in right field for a prodigious home run.

"That's the way to clout, Stan!"

"That's hitting it, Musial!"

Stan doffed his cap in rounding the bases, acknowledging the applause of the fans, but it was just the beginning.

In the fifth inning Red Schoendeinst was on base as the Man came up to bat for the third time. Leo Durocher still had Johnny Antonelli on the mound, but the way Stan hit the ball that day it wouldn't have mattered who was pitching. Musial waited for a good one, then drove it more than three hundred fifty-four feet over the top of the forty-foot pavilion in right center field. It was a tremendous drive, one of the longest home runs in his career.

Red Schoendienst scored and waited to shake Stan's hand as he crossed the plate.

"Great going, Stan!"

"You hit 'em, Stan!"

Two home runs in two consecutive times at bat is a great feat in baseball and the fans whooped it up and shouted their admiration for the great St. Louis star.

In the sixth inning, with Jim Hearn on the mound, Stan singled sharply to right for his third straight hit. It was a routine safety for Stan the Man, but the crowded park gave him the great big cheer anyway. He was the Cardinal's big man and the fans loved him. They should have saved their voices and their throats. They were going to need them later.

In the eighth inning the score was tied, 6–6. The Giants had done some team slugging on their own. Wally Moon and Red Schoendienst were on base and Jim Hearn was trying to stem the Redbird fire. Stan Musial came to bat.

"Get another hit, Stan!"

"Bang it out of here!"

Jim Hearn pitched the slugger craftily. Stan let a couple go by. Then Hearn pitched a slider. Musial liked it, stepped into the ball and drove it like a rifleshot over the Busch Stadium roof for his third big homerun of the game.

The crowd went wild.

"Yeah, Stan!"

"What a man!"

Wally Moon, Red Schoendienst, Eddie Stanky and the whole St. Louis bench were out on the field to shake the big fellow's hand.

"It's the greatest individual day any player ever had," said Stanky.

"That's hitting 'em, Stan!"

But that fabulous day wasn't over. There was more to come.

The Cardinals romped off the field with the first game of the scheduled double-header in their pockets. They were just a bunch of kids in the clubhouse between games.

"I thought you said you were just a singles hitter," they kidded their big man affectionately.

"That's what I am," answered Stan. "Just a singles hitter."

"How many home runs did Babe Ruth hit at this time of the year—when he got his big sixty?"

Stan grinned.

"They're just pitching them where I can hit them," he demurred.

"Terrific, Stan!" shouted Eddie Stanky. "Just you keep belting them and we'll tear this league apart!"

Out in the stands of the St. Louis ball park the fans were buzzing excitedly.

"Three in one game! That's a lot of home run hitting!"

"He got four for four!"

"One was a single!"

"He hit three homers!"

"What a man!"

The Cards trotted out of the clubhouse for the second game of the afternoon against the New York Giants, and the big crowd stood up to give the Man a thunderous welcome.

"Come on, Stan!"

"You're our man, Stan!"

Stan tipped his hat modestly, accepting the big welcome of the fans. He was going to tip that hat a few more times to more rousing cheers as the sun began to set that afternoon over Busch Stadium in St. Louis.

Don Liddle opened on the hill for the Giants in the second game, and again, as in the first game, Stan drew a walk in the first inning and scored.

In the third inning, with Liddle still pitching, Stan caught hold of a fast one and the stadium was up on its feet with the crack of the bat. It was a hard, powerful, long drive. It traveled four hundred and ten feet. But the amazing Willie Mays, one of the fastest men in baseball, raced back to dead center, almost to the wall of the stadium, and the fans groaned as he pulled it in.

"Should have pulled it, Stan!" let out a disappointed fan. "It would have been another home run."

"Ten more feet!" yelled another disappointed rooter.

But Stan was going to make up for that disappointment.

Don Liddle had gone out for a pinch hitter in the big eight-run fourth inning. The Giants were leading 8–3 and their ace relief hurler was pitching when Stan got up to the plate in the fifth inning. Red Schoendienst was on base and the big crowd began to plead with Stan to do something.

"We want a hit!"

"Belt it, Stan!"

That's exactly what the Man did.

Hoyt Wilhelm is a knuckle ball artist. He pitches the kind of ball which can take off in any direction. It's a difficult pitch to hit squarely. Most of the hits off a knuckle ball pitcher are pop-ups or scratch hits.

Stan watched a couple of Wilhelm's knucklers break around the plate. Then the Giant hurler tossed on in, and Stan stepped in and whaled the ball clear out of the park and into Grand Avenue. It was a prodigious clout. It scored Red Schoendienst ahead of him. It was his fourth home run of the day and the St. Louis crowd went wild.

"That's hitting them, Stan! Wow! Four homers in a day!"

"That's belting the ball, Stan!"

In the dugout Red Schoendienst slapped the big back of his roommate.

"One more home run and you're in the record book!"

The rookie Cardinals, who had already been sufficiently awed by their big man, popped their eyes in anticipation.

"Stan Musial has just tied a major league record!" blared the public address system to the still-cheering fans in Busch Stadium. "Stan Musial has just hit his fourth home run! That is the major league record for home runs in a double-header!"

The noise in the stadium swelled to deafening proportions in tribute to the great slugger.

"See what I mean?" said Schoendienst, shouting to be heard above the noise.

"Break it, Stan!" urged Solly Hemus.

"You can do it, Stan!" said Wally Moon.

"Hit it!" pleaded the fans, as Stan stepped up to the plate in the seventh inning.

"Bang it out of here!" yelled the fans.

They were up on their feet and hollering before Stan could take his first cut against Hoyt Wilhelm, who was still on the mound for the New York Club.

Hoyt had pitched one home run ball to the slugger. He pitched carefully.

Stan watched his every move. For once he was really going to go after that home run blast. The spirit of the club, the spirit of the fans, had moved into him. He wanted that fifth home run, too. He wanted to break the record!

"Come on, Stan!" yelled Red Schoendienst.

"Get a good one!" yelled Eddie Stanky.

Again Stan watched while a couple of Wilhelm's knuckler balls danced around the plate. And then he stepped into the ball and there was a loud crack at the plate as the Man's big bat met the tantalizing curve and smashed it on a line, high and far and deep over the right center field wall and out of the park.

The din in the stadium was terrific!

Strangers hugged each other out of sheer excitement!

"That Man Stan!"

For the fifth time in the afternoon the great Stan Musial had banged the ball out of the game for a solid home run!

The Cardinal bench mobbed him at the plate. Even the men who played in a New York Giant uniform had to stop to applaud and admire the magnificent St. Louis slugger.

What a ballplayer, thought Leo Durocher.

"What a man!" said Willie Mays.

The lights were on in Busch Stadium. It was just five minutes short of eight o'clock when Stan came up in the ninth inning, but the crowd hadn't budged. They were waiting around to see whether Stan was going to hit another one.

Larry Jansen was pitching and this time all Stan could do was to pop out, but the noise which greeted that easy fly has rarely if ever been matched in baseball history.

No one, not even the Mighty Babe Ruth, had ever hit five home runs in one day. That feat was accomplished by the man who will one day join Babe Ruth in the Hall of Fame—Stan Musial.

CHAPTER 27

The Giant pitchers walked Stan four times in the game which followed his history-making home run exhibition, and no one but the St. Louis fans could blame them. Even the Cardinal fans, for all their howling protest, could understand the reason for the Giants' fears. Musial was baseball's greatest batter.

There were other records Stan had set for himself.

"I'd like to meet Rogers Hornsby's record for seven batting championships. I'd like to meet Honus Wagner's record of nine batting crowns."

The consensus of opinion among sports scribes is that Stan, who is only thirty-five years old, will not only meet those records, but beat them. He didn't do it in 1954, but there were other records he made and broke in that big season.

On August 21st Musial came in with a game-winning tally against the Cincinnati Redlegs. This was his one hundredth run of the season. It extended the record he had himself established in 1953. Stan now had scored one hundred or more runs for St. Louis in eleven consecutive seasons.

The next day, August 22nd, Stan belted two doubles to lead his club to a 9–7 triumph over the Cincinnati club. That second double hiked his total bases collected for the season to three hundred and one, and again the Man had extended a record he had established in 1953. For the tenth time in his major league playing career Stan had belted the ball for three hundred or more total bases in one season.

On August 29th, playing against the New York Giants, the Man drove out his thirty-second double of the season. This was his five hundredth as a big-league player, and it put him into that small club of major-leaguers with five hundred doubles in lifetime records. Once more Stan was among the baseball elite: Tris Speaker, Ty Cobb, Honus Wagner, Napoleon Lajoie, Paul Waner, Charlie Gehringer, Harry Heilman, Rogers Hornsby, Joe Medwick, Al Simmons, Lou Gehrig, Joe Cronin, Ed Delehanty, Babe Ruth, Goose Goslin. It is quite a club!

Stan didn't win the batting crown in 1954, but he was way up there, of course, and close to it. The Man had hit well over .300 for every year of his major league history. In 1954 he banged out one hundred and ninety-five hits, thirty-five home runs and came home with a big batting average of .330.

There are several good years of baseball ahead for Musial. There are many more records he will make for the game. The bat which cracked out those five record-making home runs on May 2, 1954, is now on display up in Cooperstown, N. Y., in the Hall of Fame. It is only a matter of time before Stan Musial's name will be enrolled in that roster of immortal baseball men.

"I've got several good years left as an active player," said Stan at a recent baseball gathering. "I'll feel that I've reached my highest goal, my greatest ambition, when I reach the 3,000 hit mark. I figure it will take me about three more years to hit that goal, and with luck I'll join a charmed circle of baseball stars like Ty Cobb, Tris Speaker, Hans Wagner, Nap Lajoie, Eddie Collins, Cap Anson and Paul Waner."

"When I hit that mark," said Musial, wistfully, "then I'll think seriously of retiring as an active Cardinal ball player. . . ."

Meanwhile there are the seasons ahead, seasons in which Stan Musial will continue to dazzle the eyes of the fans with the brilliance of his play, and seasons in which, no doubt, Stan Musial will manage the St. Louis Cardinals or another team to pennant flags and World Series championships. He has all the talent and ability to be a great manager. If anyone at all today can be called Mr. Baseball, it is the man who came up from the poor mill town of Donora, Pennsylvania, to electrify the baseball world with his consistently great batting, his modest, unassuming and inspiring team play, with his big hand and his big heart, Stanley Frank Musial.

INDEX